TENGWE

GARDEN

CLUB

My Story of Zimbabwe

Ann Rothrock Beattie

ISBN 978-0-6152-0073-6

Printed in the United States of America by Lulu Press

Prologue

The Tengwe Garden Club Annual General Meeting of 2001 may have been the most memorable gathering at my house on Katengwe Farm. Now that's saying a lot. I had many memorable parties, but this one stands out to me, more now than then, as a scene that highlights the spirited essence of the now displaced and obsolete community I loved so deeply.

Serena and I were forced to plan the meeting a little differently that year from previous years. The traditional variety of booths selling homemade goods, plants, Christmas trinkets and such, several raffles and a big to-do at the club seemed unfitting amongst turmoil, so we planned a lunch and a meeting to be held in my garden. My house was the chosen setting for several reasons – I would like to say that the stunning rose garden was the draw, but really the absence of drunk, screaming and chanting "war vets" at my gate was the main reason. We were not about to let them ruin our day – *we* would be the only drunk and screaming people around!

The day was a typical December day, hot and sunny, no humidity and fortunately for us, but surely to our husbands' disappointment, no rain. Louie and Irene unpacked the "tea trunk," an old dented black, metal army trunk that traveled with the secretary to all garden club meetings. It was full of enough tea cups, saucers, spoons, sugar bowls and tea pots for the entire garden club. The ladies arrived mid-morning for tea and those with babies and toddlers set up "day-care" under the shade of the cassia trees near the guest cottage, with Irene in charge as head nanny. It was a manageable number of kids, probably around thirty or so, as the weekly boarders were not home yet for Christmas break. Only the children under age five came to the meeting. And of course, no one was foolish enough to leave her nanny behind for a festive event like this.

As it was the year-end meeting, the main objective was to elect new officers. Se and I had been chairlady and secretary for two years running and were hoping for replacements. I was definitely stepping down; Dave and I had made a plan months before not to grow a tobacco crop that season and do some traveling in an attempt to determine if we could possibly settle somewhere other than our endangered little heaven. Having returned from a six week journey through South Africa, we were home for the holidays and then were off to the States in January for a few months. The general state of uncertainty was obvious, as there were no forthcoming offers to commit to a year's responsibility, albeit Garden Club.

I don't remember who actually suggested it, but the idea of Tengwe Garden Club taking a year off came up and was knocked around a bit – until one of the more outspoken "old tops" stood up and gave us youngsters nothing short of a scolding lecture. She cited the fact that this garden club had been going strong for almost forty years, since its inception at the prompting of Rosa Hinde, ironically Dave's grandmother. ("Old tops" is not a degrading term at all. In fact, it is quite an endearing term for the respected older generation, also referred to as "toppies" for short.) And these toppies had surely seen trying times before this, so how on earth were we going to let the Tengwe Garden Club fall by the wayside after all this time – well, the message got through and we instantly had a full roster of new officers! Even women already stretched too thin with other committee jobs jumped in to keep the club alive.

The meeting adjourned and the wine flowed. We served an exquisite lunch, a collaborative effort, the likes of which the Tengwe ladies had become famous for: Lemon Chicken (can't top the one from "Silver Palate"), my unbeatable broccoli salad, Debbie's Potato Bake, Sue's

Mediterranean Salad, Serena's Chocolate Mousse and Gill's Apple Delight. I had concocted some watermelon punch that I can recall being extremely potent, and it went down very quickly. So there we were, lunching and sipping and chatting away, probably forty to fifty women of all ages, with children running all over the place or hanging out of the mango and litchie trees – everyone having an absolute ball.

After dessert and more wine, my mother-in-law could see where this was headed and mercifully whisked my son James, age three, away to her house for the night, half a mile away. As the music cranked and a massive "pungwe" ensued, we decided to radio all the husbands to join us. They arrived after finishing the day's tobacco farming and mealie planting to find very happy wives. Lunch rolled into dinner. I had Louie pull out all the steaks and "borewors" from the deep freeze and roast some potatoes while Never lit the "braii" for a good ole Zimbabwean cookout. We fed about fifty or sixty people that night with the men in charge of the grill and the girls in the kitchen. The nannies and children were fed and put to bed in the cozy beds the back of the truck always transformed into at night. My yard turned into a virtual parking lot full of sleeping children all close by so we could hear any chirps from the babes. It must have been right after dinner that we broke out the ABBA – usually Mandy's request – and we danced until midnight, not letting any CD go unplayed. This was a party complete with Debbie's rendition of "Time Warp," Pete Mason's Irish Coffees, Andy Kockott pulling the girls' hair, Douglas' Impala Dance, and Gillie's slurring and giggling.

Anyone watching this scene from outside would not have heard the inevitable turn in conversation to "what are your plans?" or "where will you go if...?" or "we're going to wait and see." Anyone watching from outside would not predict the impending massive upheaval about to fall upon this community. Anyone watching from outside would have seen a group from all walks of life, bonded together by friendships, old and new, who knew the importance of community, the commitment to family and friends, and the love of a land embedded so deeply in all of us.

It has been five years since we left Zimbabwe, left our beloved farm, left the best friends we've ever known, and worst of all left our family. I look back on my time there and know now that it changed me in so many ways. In my farewell speech to our friends I told them through my tears that "…The decision to move to Tengwe was the easiest one of my life. The decision to leave Tengwe, however, has by far been the most difficult. … I can honestly say that my time here has made me a better person, and I have all of you to thank for that. You have taught me a level of friendship, kindness and compassion that I will take with me forever."

When I fell in love with Dave, I had no idea what life had in store for me. Too many times now I have tried to answer the questions of how one African safari trip changed the course of my life, but have never had the opportunity to tell the story the way I want to. Here is my story....

PART ONE

SAFARI

Chapter 1

By August 1995, I was absolutely certain of the direction my life would take. Having graduated from St. Catherine's School in Richmond, Va. and UNC Chapel Hill, I had moved directly to New York City, which had been my plan ever since the summer before my senior year at college, during which time I spent one fantastic summer in the city waiting tables at Rockefeller Center. I began a love affair with New York, as so many young people do, and thrived on the energy and excitement it provides. I reluctantly returned to Chapel Hill to finish college, counting the days until I could reunite with my beloved city and enter the real world. I flatly refused to entertain any ideas of post-grad activity like my brother who was in law school – I wanted New York, period.

At the time of my college graduation, my father had been dead for eight months. My mother was still very much the grieving widow, trying to come to terms with the events of the past few years of her own life. Since I was about fifteen, my mother, brother and I had begun the emotionally and mentally bruising process of admitting my alcoholic father into one rehab center after another around the state. My participation in this was limited by the fact that I was away at boarding school, a circumstance I know my mother was grateful for and quite truthfully, so was I. By the time my brother Aubrey and I were in college (both at UNC), Dad's condition had deteriorated to the point of complete futility. Being closer to our home in High Point, NC, meant that my involvement in his addiction and its repercussions increased, and I found myself once driving home in the middle of the night to help Mom clean up a bloody mess after Dad had fallen down the stairs, cracked his head open and left the guest room looking like a slaughterhouse. He was rushed to the emergency room and once again began another drying-out session in the hospital. These little spells in the hospital, in addition to the four treatment centers, were incredibly expensive and since Dad had, not surprisingly, lost his once very successful job, money was an imminent concern. I watched my mother enable to the point of her own desperation. Once, she spent a full week at a treatment center in Tarboro, as the program required the spouses to do as part of the rehabilitation process. How disappointed and crestfallen she must have been when, after many weeks and thousands of dollars were spent on recovery, my father filled the grocery cart with beer and wine on their way home. Once, Mom, Aubrey and I spent an entire Christmas Day in the emergency room. Once, to our mortification, my father showed up drunk at the illustrious "Dean Dome" in Chapel Hill for a basketball game. Finally, in September 1991, the start of my senior year in college, Dad put a bullet through his head, all at once ending the horror we lived. The three of us then began the grieving process in different ways, and truth be told, for me it was a relief.

My mother did not protest when I was accepted into the unpaid intern program at Sotheby's Auction House to begin the following summer in New York. She did not protest when I quit the subsequent boring and unchallenging job I had gotten at an art gallery after not quite a year. She did, however, protest after I had spent an entire summer unemployed but having lots of fun, all on her bill. In August 1993, Mom very deservedly splurged on herself and joined a group of friends on a safari to Kenya, her first African experience. Her last words to me as I put her on the plane at Kennedy airport went something like, "If you do not have a job by the time I come home, you are coming back to High Point with me." Well, that woke me up, and I went straight to a capable headhunter and landed a job within a week at a large, well-known wholesale fabric company. I even sent Mom a fax in Kenya to tell her the good news, and believe it or not she actually received it a week later! Mom returned from Kenya injected with new life, vowing to return to Africa one day with her children so that we, too, could have the same amazing and spectacular experience she had had. I was just thrilled to see her so renewed upon her return, never guessing the prophetic meaning hidden in her words.

I was thoroughly satisfied with my new job. It offered me the opportunity to learn the fabric business from the bottom up, travel a bit, and gain experience in the corporate world. I was not making much money, and Mom still had to supplement my income, but I got steady raises and a promotion in a short amount of time. I worked hard and dedicated many long hours, often spending weekends at the office, but I truly enjoyed what I was doing. I had been in New York long enough to really feel like it was home. I had great roommates, a fabulous apartment in the East Village, and several circles of great friends.

In June 1995, Mom called to announce that we (Mom, Aubrey, then in Washington, DC practicing law, and I) had the opportunity to join a group of friends, some old some new, on a wing-shooting safari to Zimbabwe. One thing my father did do for his family was instill the love of bird shooting in us all. I was last to come on board, but I soon realized that in my family if you did not shoot or play golf, you got left behind on most trips, and golf was out of the question. This proposed trip was the height of fulfillment for any wingshooter or outdoorsman: two weeks to shoot guinea hens, doves, francolin, sand grouse, ducks and geese with the option of plains game shooting and tiger fishing on the Zambezi River. We put our names in and the trip was booked for the last two weeks of August.

My job was still going pretty well, and it was time for my yearly review just before I was to leave for Zimbabwe; what I had been working toward for months finally came to pass. I was promoted to what was to be called the Sales Coordinator, which was big news for me, as I was ready to tackle this position with vigor and really advance my career. I left the office that day on top of the world, feeling confident that I would make it on my own in the corporate world.

And so, Mom and Aubrey flew to New York where we rendezvoused with a portion of our group and set off for our Zimbabwean safari.

Chapter 2

We boarded the South African Airways flight and thus began our journey. Mom took advantage of the fact that she had me locked in for sixteen hours straight to probe me regarding my plans. What she really was trying to determine, I am sure, was how much longer she would need to subsidize my life in New York. I was proud to announce to her that I had made great strides in my job; I was going to be a career woman; I was going to climb that corporate ladder. I was twenty-five years old with no romantic interests of any consequence at the time, and I was happy with my life and job in New York. Mom seemed mollified by my answers and, as always, was supportive and encouraging.

We arrived exhausted into Johannesburg airport where we found the remainder of our group. Our clan totaled twelve and included old and new friends of all ages. Our immediate and closest friends were Johnny and Susan Corpening, who were longtime friends from High Point. Sara Corpening, Johnny and Susan's daughter, one of identical twins I had grown up with and a great childhood buddy of mine, was also with us. The rest of the group included some more of their extended family, as well as other hunting cronies from North Carolina. Mom, Aubrey and I rounded out the group.

Our itinerary for the safari was divided into three parts:

1. Chewore Fishing Camp on the Zambezi River
2. Chisamba Hunting Lodge, located in Lion's Den
3. Sengwa Hunting Camp, located on Lake Kariba

Camp One – Chewore Fishing Camp, Zambezi River, Zimbabwe

We landed in chartered planes on a narrow, dirt air strip alongside the mighty Zambezi River mid-morning, which afforded me my first glimpse of the African bush, a sight that will forever awe and inspire me. I was overcome by the nervous excitement of landing in a far away country I had never seen, and couldn't take my eyes off the foreign landscape. The air was dry and dusty, the short thorn trees were stark with no leaves, and the Landcruisers were fitted with seats on the back, just as I had seen on TV. The camp was situated on the banks of the Zambezi River, with a breathtaking view on all sides. We divided ourselves into sleeping arrangements that best suited the make-up of the party. Chewore Fishing Camp had a few permanent lodges – A-framed thatched structures set up on top of cement flooring complete with running water, showers and toilets. Mom, Susan, Sara and I grabbed one of those and called it "Girls' Dorm."

These first days on the Zambezi were spent in pursuit of the challenging tiger fish, named for its stripes and razor sharp teeth. Our Zimbabwean safari guides at this camp tried gamely to find some fish for us, but as August is really not the best time of year for it, we struggled on this front. (In retrospect, Dave, an incredibly skilled fisherman of note in Zimbabwe, scoffs at the inability of those guides to find adequate fish for us – something we laugh about to this day!) It really didn't matter though; what we enjoyed most was the game-viewing at this spot, as it was the first time for many of us. There really is no way to prepare for the sensation of watching an elephant bull, a masterpiece of a creature, trod powerfully through thick bush that to any other would be a closed path. There are no words to accurately describe the intimidation and plain fear instilled as a fifteen foot crocodile glides soundlessly by. Nor is there a way to explain the enchanting spectacle of a herd of one hundred impala leaping gracefully through the air on pencil thin, agile legs. Nighttime in the bush brings its own set of sounds and activities: the almost comical, but endearing, grunting of the hippo that can actually rock you to sleep, and the heart-stopping, hair-raising roar of a male lion that keeps you from that sleep.

We equally enjoyed the man-made nighttime activities – sitting around the campfire, recalling the days' events, eating biltong (a sort of beef jerky, but the real thing) and exploring the fine qualities of South African wine (there are many!) The three days along the Zambezi were a fantastic introduction to the stark beauty of this country, but when the time came to go to our next camp, we all had anxious trigger fingers and were ready to hunt.

Chapter 3

Camp Two – Chisamba Hunting Camp, Lion's Den, Zimbabwe

We arrived again in two chartered planes onto dirt air strips, this time
coming onto very different terrain from that of the Zambezi Valley. This
camp was on prime farmland that was a massive farming enterprise in corn,
cattle and plains game spanning five thousand acres.

We were met by our guide Pete Fick who introduced us to the
landowner Brink Bosman and a friend Dave Beattie, who had been asked to
help out on the safari. (Now, here I have to interject. How Dave Beattie
actually came to be a part of this safari is key to my story. Dave, living in
Tengwe, about an hour away, had extensive experience as a safari guide and
big game hunter in South Africa before coming home to farm with his dad.
Pete Fick, our guide, did need assistance, but the fact that four young, single
girls were on this trip did not escape his attention, and this was indeed
possibly the best wingshooting available in the country. Dave, a bachelor
and keen birdshooter as well, would be a fool to miss out on this one!)

The staff unloaded the gear while we piled randomly into the various
Land Cruisers. Mom and I climbed in the cab of Dave's cruiser. On the thirty
minute ride to the camp, Mom chattered endlessly, asking every question she
could think of to Dave, who answered very patiently. While she kept him
distracted with her chit-chat, I had a chance to check him out and found him

handsome in his Ray-Bans and dark tanned skin, but laughed to myself at the silly "short-shorts" all the Zimbabwean men chose to wear. He dropped us at the camp where the girls claimed another rondovel (round, brick, thatched-roof lodges) and settled in. These rondovels had large arched openings that served as windows, with curtains to cover, but no glass panes as the weather did not call for it. Each twin bed had a mosquito net hanging from the ceiling to keep the pesky bugs away. We were to shoot doves that afternoon after lunch and a "kip," (i.e. nap - a wonderful routine we all became very fond of).

After a successful afternoon dove shoot, we gathered around the vehicles to drink a cold beer, count birds, and watch the mesmerizing sunset, one of Africa's most superb gifts. We headed back to camp to shower before dinner, a tricky task as there was no electricity. Candles, flashlights and paraffin lamps showed us the way, and I realized what a waste of space it was to pack all of my makeup. Fortunately, hot water was provided by a Rhodesian Boiler, a system whereby large tanks of water were kept hot by a wood-fueled fire. The first night in Lions Den was a festive one, where we got to know our guide, Pete, and Johnny kept us entertained with tasteless jokes, as is his custom. Dave had gone home to Tengwe, as he had "bar duty," a job I was to become very familiar with in the future, but meant nothing to me at the time, just that he couldn't join us for dinner that night. He would be back in the morning for the driven shoot.

At sunrise, we were off for driven shoots of francolin, guineas, and doves. I had not experienced this type of shoot before and was fascinated to see how a line of beaters could successfully herd hundreds of birds towards a line of shooters. The beaters' line was comprised of about thirty natives (men, women and children), who began about a mile away from the shooters, walking towards us, making loud hooting calls and beating the bushes with sticks, in order to flush the birds our way. We waited for the onslaught of fast-flying birds to come overhead. The saying "If it flies, it dies" was our motto; unfortunately, one of our less experienced shooters took this to the extreme and unknowingly shot a three-banded courser, a bird which never should have seen a bullet. On one driven shoot, Aubrey and I were next to each other in the line and, as the birds were being driven, so were about fifty sable that stampeded so closely my hair flapped in their wake, and in between us so swiftly that we did nothing but stand and stare at these magnificent creatures running by. After that, all we could do was to stand frozen and wide-eyed, so stunned that we missed the entire flock of guineas flying safely overhead.

Our days (five in total) at Chisamba followed a routine that started with early morning shoots, a late brunch and usually a Bloody Mary or two, which tied in nicely with the "kip after lunch" custom. Tea was served around three o'clock before returning to the field for an afternoon shoot until sundown, then back to camp for showers, drinks around the campfire, and dinner in the large thatched-roof dining lodge. As I said, the first night, Dave did not join us, but true to his word, the next morning he was there showing us where to stand, executing the driven shoots, and helping us spot the birds with his ever-keen eyesight. His professional ability was obvious, and we all benefited from his expertise in the field.

The second night in camp Dave had planned to stay on so that he would be around for the early morning hunt. As was custom, we had drinks around the campfire, while everyone drilled Dave about his background (I believe Pete's had been thoroughly covered the night before). The complex history of Zimbabwe had dictated much of Dave's early life; as a young man of eighteen in 1976, he was required to engage in the bloody civil war for what was then the Rhodesian army, fighting to maintain white control over the black majority. International politicians finally ended the "chimurenga" (meaning struggle) by placing enough political pressure on the South

African government to cut off their Rhodesian ally. Ian Smith's white regime was forced to make the inevitable transition to black government for the newly named country of Zimbabwe in 1980. Dave had been a player in the war as a member of the police, but after the war, he found his true calling as a wildlife ranger in Hwange National Park in western Zimbabwe. After several years it became increasingly apparent that an aggressive indigenization program by the new government would make it difficult to continue in a career of this nature. He moved on to South Africa, where he worked as a safari guide at Mala Mala, a well-known safari lodge, and eventually as a professional hunter for a private outfitter, where he worked for about five years before returning to Zimbabwe.

He kept us engrossed in conversation that night with his tales of Africa and dangerous big-game hunting stories, until it was very late and the group started to peel off to bed. I found myself sitting alone with Dave at one end of the long dining table. Never being one to shy away from a scotch, I accepted as Dave poured. We talked that night at that table until long after midnight – we swapped stories about our lives as though we were not strangers at all, but long-time friends. He told me about his brief, two year marriage upon his return to Tengwe, which ended in divorce. He talked passionately about his daughter, Kimi, age five at the time. I told him about my life in New York, my job, and my family. The time ticked away until the scotch was empty, we were both yawning, and we realized the wake-up call was coming in a few hours, so we said a friendly goodnight.

Sara was quick to question me the next morning about any romantic interludes the previous night (we had swapped "boy stories" many times in the past), but I simply told her the truth about our interesting, and innocent, talk. She gave a knowing smile but did not press.

I had been personally frustrated with my shooting skills up to that point. That day Dave, detecting my discouragement, stood with me and patiently pointed out my mistakes. Before the end of the day, I was much improved and confident again, just in time for one the best hunts of the trip – we shot 220 guineas that day at a place aptly named Hamburger Hill. By sundown that day, the group was pumped up by our hunting success, and we sat around, drinking beer in the field while the numerous birds were counted and the sun set. I watched Dave open my beer that afternoon, and swear to this day it was one of the things that attracted me to him from the beginning. There is no such thing as a twist-off bottle cap in Zimbabwe, so he just held one bottle cap at the perfect angle against another one, and with one quick jerk, the cap popped off. My hands bled as I tried desperately to do it, but failed, and was convinced that no Manhattan city boy could ever pull that trick off either. We arrived back at camp that night after dark, and as I jumped off the back of the cruiser, Dave came around to help and gave me a subtle, but bold, pat on my rear end, which sent my heart racing as this was truly the first physical gesture yet between us. I answered with a coy and flirtatious smile as I went off to shower before dinner.

We had fallen comfortably into the daily routine by this point, and it was apparent that the early mornings were taking a toll, as most of our party would bid goodnight after dessert. That third night, Mom, a retired grammar teacher, did us the favor of boring everyone with a grammar lesson in the proper use of "lay" and "lie," and Dave and I found ourselves alone at a much earlier hour than normal. We took our drinks out to the campfire and talked – oh, that accent! – until Dave (finally!) learned over and kissed me so gently and perfectly, and at that moment I felt the true intensity of our attraction. We kissed passionately by the fire that night for hours, until we reluctantly said goodnight. Avoiding the door, so as to not disturb my roommates, I climbed through the arched opening of our rondovel and fell onto my bed, as it was directly underneath the window, so tired I did not even pull the mosquito net down around me.

The wake-up call that morning came very quickly, and as I was lacing up my shoes, I saw Mom's feet and felt her hovering over me. The conversation went like this: Mom said, "Just what were you doing until three o'clock in the morning?" I said, "Moooom, we were **just** talking!" Mom said, "Well, I want you to know that Dave is a **very** experienced man." And so with that, I ran straight to Dave to tell him what Mom had just said. He still claims it was the best thing she could have done for him, convinced her comments may have piqued my interest and curiosity in him even more!

We continued to have wonderful game viewing and shooting at Lions Den, and Dave was extremely professional throughout the trip, paying equal attention to all of us in the day, but at night we belonged only to each other. That fourth night was surely one of the most unforgettable ones I will ever know. Dave pulled a mattress out after everyone had gone to bed, and we slept by the water, under the majestic African sky. Once again, we spent hours kissing and cuddling – nothing more. Nothing less. We slept off and on, my head nestled perfectly on his shoulder. The connection we felt was so natural that to deny it would have in some way been abnormal behavior. I had never before known the security and peace I found in his strong, sure arms.

The fifth day brought anxiety for me, as I knew the following day we were to leave for the third and final camp at Lake Kariba, many miles from Lions Den. The planes were scheduled to arrive the next morning, and I couldn't bear the thought of having to say goodbye to Dave. It seemed fate was on our side. As it turned out, because of the added weight of the guns and ammo, our group needed three planes to transport us to the next camp instead of the usual two. As this would have been an added cost, a plan was proposed for Dave to drive his truck to the third camp, loaded with luggage and gear, thus sparing us the expense of a third plane. This also meant that Dave could join us for the remaining four days of our safari. Everyone voted for that, as Dave had not only stolen my heart, but the rest of the group's as well. Because of his background as a hunting guide and his excellent fishing ability, Dave was able to connect with our entire group. One lady in our group shared his love of fishing, and they would often eschew the lunchtime kip and catch a bass or a bream on the dam by the camp.

Dave and I realized in an instant this drive was a golden opportunity for us to be alone for a whole day. I announced that I was riding with him on the eight hour drive to begin at dawn the next morning.

Chapter 4

Camp Three, Sengwa Safari Camp, Lake Kariba, Zimbabwe

We left very early that morning with a full truck and one African tracker to help show us the way. We went through a town called Karoi to do some shopping on the way, my first introduction to daily life in Africa. The store was remarkably well stocked – I had envisioned something far more basic. We were able to stock up on Dewar's Scotch, Bloody Mary fixings, South African wine, fresh fruit and vegetables to take to the next camp. I wandered through the aisles to get a taste of the local foods and was fascinated by the massive bags of corn meal stacked against one wall. I was keenly aware of the rank smell of body odor of the natives, who have no regard for personal space and crowd each other to the point of touching. I was blown away by the nauseating stench that hit me as I approached the kapenta section (little dried fish), apparently a favorite of the locals. The unsliced loaves of white bread sat, uncovered, on metal racks for anyone to touch while people grabbed and bagged the loaves themselves. Eggs could be bought by the dozen, or one at a time, but I was surprised to find they were not displayed in the refrigerated section. In contrast, Kellogg cereals and all the Nestle products were readily available. Fruit Loops, Frosted Flakes, Nescafe and Tabasco lined the shelves. Though the store was quite crowded and chaotic, I was impressed that we were able to do our errands with relative ease and even grab a bacon and egg roll on the way for breakfast. This particular drive was down the length of Lake Kariba, a man-made lake two hundred miles long, on a dusty dirt road the whole way. During the long journey we had plenty of time to talk – believe it or not, it was on this journey that we actually learned each other's last names! Somehow it had not really mattered.

The rest of the group had flown and were to arrive at camp around lunchtime. They were looking for us around three o'clock or so in time for the afternoon duck shoot, but we decided to take our time and enjoy the adventure. Mom, an avid journaler, wrote on that day, "Ann arrived too late with Dave for this drive…Where have they been?!" As it turned out, we had the entire camp to ourselves for the afternoon. We took a stroll and enjoyed the exquisite sunset over Lake Kariba. Dave told me about his house on the lake, and for the first time, we discussed the possibility of a future trip when he would take me there. I believe we both knew the improbability of that, but the idea of a final goodbye in three days time was unthinkable.

The next day was Dave's thirty-seventh birthday, Aug 25. Susan and Sara, quite the chefs, surprised him with a homemade cake which they had cooked themselves after commandeering the camp kitchen and showing off their kitchen savvy, and we celebrated in style until late in the evening. Dave and I had continued with our "sleeping under the stars" tradition, and on that night, our seven day anniversary, we finally made love under the glow of a full moon and the Southern Cross. It was simply the natural progression in our relationship and was as sweet an act of love as I ever hope to know.

Our last days on Lake Kariba were an extremely fulfilling African safari experience. We saw hundreds of Cape buffalo, we were surrounded by hippo and crocodiles, and the majestic Fish Eagle kept us fascinated with his distinctive call and immense wingspan. The warthogs came into camp, and the impala, kudu and waterbuck put on a fabulous display for us. The duck and goose shooting was bountiful. Egyptian geese, white-faced ducks (whistlers), cape shovelers, knob-billed ducks and the impressive spurwing goose were all in our bag.

The planes arrived to take us back to Harare on Sunday morning. Fortunately someone else drove Dave's car so that he could fly with us. We entered into pandemonium at the Harare airport – quite a shock after two tranquil weeks in the bush – and certainly not an environment conducive to an emotional goodbye. My tears and sobs were uncontrollable, and even more so when Dave told me he loved me. I managed "I love you, too" somehow, and then he was gone.

Just like that.

I was instantly thrown back into a reality I did not want and felt the weight of a long plane ride and work the next day heavily on my shoulders. How was I now supposed to go back to my life? Was I meant to label this interlude a "safari romance" and place it neatly in my past? Mom's final quote in her journal was, "Ann & Dave – a serious thing?!?!" My question exactly, Mom!

Chapter 5

The flight home was definitely long, but the most grueling part was the schedule that had me slated to be back in the office the day we landed at seven o'clock in the morning. A quick shower and I was off to work, where I spent most of the day sitting at my desk, pretending to go through the pile of work that had waited for me. My great friend and co-worker, Andrea, surprised me by picking up immediately on a change in my demeanor. She couldn't wait to get all the details over lunch, and I couldn't wait to tell them! I already felt so far away from Dave, that any opportunity to speak his name somehow brought him closer.

The next morning I went to work early, when my roommate called to say I had missed a call from Dave shortly after I had left the apartment, and I was unable to concentrate for the entire day. This long-distance relationship carried on for the next few weeks, with phone calls at irregular hours. The seven hour time difference made things difficult, not to mention that Dave was on an unreliable party-line system on the farm.

I was increasingly distracted at work, and struggled to recapture the motivation and ambition that had consumed me only two weeks prior to my return. All of a sudden, the corporate world did not seem so glamorous and attractive in my eyes after all, but instead took on a monotonous and obligatory role.

Dave and I tried to make plans for future travel, but as I was out of vacation days and it was mid-summer on the farm, we struggled to figure out how we would see each other again. After six weeks of this, I decided to take the bull by the horns and worked up the nerve to suggest that I could come back to Zimbabwe for a while. When Dave responded with eager encouragement, we decided to go forward.

My biggest stumbling block then was informing my mother of my plan. I called and told her to sit down, that I had big news. She was dead silent while I explained how Dave and I still had very strong feelings for each other, and we wanted the chance to see what our relationship was really made of. She was silent while I explained that I might need help paying off a few credit cards and that I would need a plane ticket. When she did speak, she said, "I need to think about this and call you back." Thankfully, Mom knew how serious I was, and eventually agreed to help me make it happen. Dave had called her to assure her that if things did not work out at any time in the next few months, he would see me safely back on a plane home.

I did not realize that Aubrey would prove to be an even bigger stumbling block than Mom, but in my father's absence he had taken on a paternal role and confronted me with difficult questions like "Where will you live?," "Where will you work?" and "How will you have money?" I had no answers for those questions. I had absolutely no idea what I was going into, and I didn't care that I didn't know, I just knew I had to be with Dave. The question most people were too polite to ask – "What if it doesn't work out?" – didn't bother me too much.

Looking back now on that decision, I can clearly see I was a girl so in love I had no option but to take that chance and follow my heart. I don't know where it came from, but I am so grateful that I found the courage to make that leap of faith. I gave notice to a stunned boss, rented out my room, and packed my bags. On December 2, 1995, a little less than three months after leaving Dave, I boarded the same flight back to Johannesburg and back to the man I had told many I thought I might marry.

PART TWO

REUNION

Chapter 1

I wore by black Guess jeans, a white t-shirt, a denim long-sleeve shirt and cowboy boots for the plane ride – my "skinny" outfit. I purposefully put my wet hair in a bun for the trip, knowing I could let it down looking fresher when I arrived sixteen hours later. I did not sleep a wink on that flight, and I could not concentrate on a book. I filled the hours trying to imagine what I was walking into, but could not get a visual. Despite a little anxiety, I was not scared or worried, only eager to be with Dave once again so that he could make it all O.K.

I recall struggling to push my very heavy duffle bags (I had paid for extra weight), through the arrival gate, when Dave walked up to me seemingly from nowhere and we were together again. We looked at each other in amazement, doubting it was really happening, but smiles so big and hands shaking so much that we knew it was.

The first day was slightly awkward, as we were guests of some of Dave's old friends in Johannesburg and I felt a little out of place. When we could steal some time alone, fortunately all was as natural as we had remembered. Dave had driven to Johannesburg with his great childhood friend and neighbor Pete Mason, the first of the Tengwe crowd I would meet. He charmed me immediately with his wit and humor; little did I know then that he and his wife, Serena, would become two of my very best friends.

We spent two days in Johannesburg and left before dawn on the third day in order to get home to Tengwe the same day. Only then did I realize what a sacrifice it had been for Dave to drive to South Africa to pick me up – he had not hesitated when I had casually asked if he could meet me in Johannesburg to avoid the expense of another ticket. Had I known I was asking him to drive fifteen hours, I certainly would have reconsidered the request!

I experienced my first border-crossing that day at Beitbridge. Third-world customs and immigration are possibly the world's finest examples of complete disorganization in government; those who have endured this process know to allow a minimum of three hours to get through by car. The heat, the flies, and the masses of humanity make for a pretty miserable entry to this beautiful country. We managed to survive though and drove on, and on, and on, until we pulled into the farm around nine o'clock that night. I was so anxious to see everything, but it was dark and raining as we unloaded. Dave and Pete were absolutely thrilled with the rain, but I could not understand then why they were so excited. It did not take long for me to realize how crucial the rain was to our livelihood – this was a farm, after all!

It was obvious from first glance that Dave had been a bachelor for four years by the time I arrived. He lived in a sprawling, badly built, three bedroom brick farmhouse, with no décor at all. In the living room he had a beautiful set of four animal drawings, one hung on each wall. There were bookshelves stacked with yellowed fishing magazines and hunting books, and a mounted tiger fish hanging over the fireplace. The worn, threadbare furniture looked like it was decades old (turned out it was!). The kitchen was lit by one ceiling light-bulb which illuminated three makeshift cupboards with varying countertop colors. (I was informed weeks later that Dave's mother had insisted he put a ceiling in the kitchen before I arrived, a favor I was forever grateful for). The master bedroom had a mustard colored carpet and an ugly brown bedspread, and the "dining room table" sat two. Most of the windows had unattractive metal burglar bars on them, a fact of life in Zimbabwe. The cement flooring throughout the house was harsh and begged for rugs and carpeting.

The appalling décor and disrepair of the house amused me, but bothered me not at all. We dumped my bags in the room and settled in for our first night together. I remember it so vividly – Dave put on the sexy "Simply Red - Life" CD, and we made the most passionate love we had yet that night. Being back in each other's arms again was as magical as I had anticipated. We woke the next morning still clinging to each other.

I had barely gotten dressed when I heard voices, but couldn't figure out where they were coming from. I walked out of the room and was overwhelmed by the staff that awaited me in the kitchen. Dave was talking on what looked like a walkie-talkie to his mother, who was desperate to come over and meet me. The day started very early on the farm – sunrise was the appointed time for the employees to be at work – so by the time I surfaced at nine o'clock, everyone was well into the day. I was somewhat confused, and tried to pretend that I knew what was going on, but really I had no idea what life on a rural tobacco farm in Zimbabwe was like.

I met Louie, the cook, Irene, the nanny, and Clever, the garden boy. Louie was an older, petite man, with little hair on his head, and a large grin. He was dressed in a crisp white linen uniform of pants and a button down shirt. Irene was obviously young, also petite, and wore an ethnically decorated maid's dress with a scarf on her head. She gave me a shy smiled that revealed buck teeth. Clever stood at the door, not allowed in the house, and was dressed in a garden boy's uniform of blue overalls and a cap. Even though he was at the back door, I could smell his body odor from where I stood. Irene spoke a little English, Louie spoke even less, and Clever spoke none at all, but the Shona accent threw me off completely and I could not understand a word they said. I was met with much curiosity from the house staff, as well as the rest of the workforce force. Most of the families living on Dendera Farm had been there for generations and had known Dave from his childhood.

Dave's parents, Shirley and Andy Beattie, and his younger sister, Karyn, arrived shortly after the radio call, and I had my first introduction to "tea." We all sat in the living room and Louie promptly placed a tea tray on the table in front of me. We were chatting away, when I realized everyone sort of looking at the tea tray and then at me, when Dave came to my rescue and poured tea for everyone. It took me a while to catch on to the whole ritual, but basically tea-time is at ten o'clock in the morning and then again at three-thirty or four o'clock in the afternoon. Traditional practice held that anyone who arrived at my house, unannounced and unexpected, would still be welcomed for tea. I would then pour tea or coffee, serve any cake or biscuits (cookies), and chat for an hour. At first, I could not get used to the intrusion, but after a while, I came to enjoy the impromptu visits, and did not find them intrusive at all. I even dropped in on others from time to time.

I had an enlightening conversation with Shirley and Andy, who lived on the farm about a half-mile away. They had been on Dendera Farm, named for the original dense population of ground hornbills (Dendera in the Shona language), for almost forty years at the time. Andy had purchased the land from the British government in 1961 and had carved his farm out of a tract of land that was two thousand acres of thick African bush. He built roads, dams, houses, fences, workshops and tobacco barns. He built up a successful farming enterprise over the next forty years that included a large herd of cattle, cut flowers for export (mainly proteas), and tobacco and maize crops 150 acres in size. He had acquired Katengwe Farm next door during a time of expansion, where Dave's house was located. The year I arrived was to be his last; Andy would retire after that season and Dave would take over all the cropping on the farm, set up under a lease agreement. Until that point, Dave had farmed with his dad as the manager.

After they left, I was faced with a massive unpacking job. I quickly used up the ten or so spare coat-hangers in Dave's closet and asked if there were any more. That afternoon a large stack of hangers was delivered to the house and Dave explained that his electrician, named Gift, had been given the task of making me coat hangers from a coil of wire all day!

Over the next few days, I settled in and rearranged the house a bit. One day, Dave walked in to find me struggling to move a heavy piece of furniture and looked at me in disbelief. "The staff is getting bored. Why don't you give them something to do?" he said. I then asked them to move the furniture (using lots of hand gestures), and they were genuinely pleased and proud to be helping. To my surprise, they addressed me as "Madam!" Not until later did I discover that it was traditional practice of the natives to address their employers as "Boss" or "Madam." I even had to learn to refer to Dave as "the Boss" when speaking with my staff.

Having a staff was so different for me, and it took me some time to get used to having so many people in the house all day. After a while, I realized how crucial they were to running a house like ours. There were chickens which provided eggs and needed to be fed and a boiler which provided hot water and needed to be lit and kept burning. The laundry was all done by hand and every item of clothing and linen had to be ironed to avoid maggots (more on this later), the garden was about three acres, and we had five dogs. Constant sweeping throughout the day was necessary to keep up with the dirt and dust of farm life.

I was initially intimidated and overwhelmed by the size of my garden, but when I first beheld Shirley's magnificent yard, I realized that our grounds were quite small by comparison. The green fauna of December hid the stark landscape I had remembered from my first trip during the dry season. Brilliant, red flamboyant trees lined the fence down one side of the garden that was a colorful and clever display of Shirley's extensive knowledge and talent. Perfectly manicured lawn amongst palm trees, msasa trees, mfuti trees, and banana trees all surrounded the numerous flower beds chock-full of a vast variety of blooms. Strelitzias, in fiery orange, cosmos in several shades of purple, cannas in bright red and agapanthas in deep periwinkle to name a few, all served as stunning eye-candy, but the formal English rose garden at the bottom of the yard near the Dendera dam confirmed that this well-established garden was the prideful result of many years of keen attention. I was instantly inspired to learn as much as I could from her. Upon my arrival, Dave's garden had not been given much attention for some time. I could see that I had my work cut out for me.

Prior to my arrival, Sam, Dave's black lab, had a litter of puppies and he had promised one for me. My puppy was christened "Bella" upon my arrival. It had been such a long time since I had had a pet, not to mention five, and I was thrilled to have dogs again. The motley crew included Sam, the black lab, Bella, her puppy, Freckles, an old, limping pointer, Cindy, a fox terrier and Jock, a mixed breed of unknown origin.

Louie was patient with me for a few days, and then one morning after breakfast, asked me what I wanted him to cook for lunch. It was definitely time for me to take over the menu, as we had been eating bacon and eggs for breakfast and steak and chips (fries) for lunch the first week I was there, and I knew my body could not handle Dave's bachelor food. He agreed that we could eat healthier and took me to Karoi, the closest grocery store, thirty miles away, the exact store I had experienced on the safari. Little did I know on that day this was to become my mainstay grocery store! I learned that meat was purchased separately from a butchery. In Karoi, a butchery called Buffalo Downs was located just outside town on a cattle farm. I was at first repelled by all the raw meat lying all over the place. The pungent odor of freshly slaughtered cattle and pigs shocked me as we entered. A long counter with one cash register was all that separated us from carcasses waiting to be chopped. They sold all the cuts of meats, if you knew what to ask for, as it was generally not displayed. Most of the meat was stored in large freezers. I let Dave order for us the first time and listened intently while he asked for mince (hamburger meat), rump (similar to sirloin), several chickens and beef fillet (pronounced "fill-it"). I learned that no part of a cow went to waste – any off-cuts were sold as either "ration-meat," a sort of stewing beef which I bought for the staff, or "pets meat," which was the absolute dregs and too nasty to even feed the dogs in my opinion. In the end I also bought them ration meat, for the pets' meat was way too smelly! We walked out with a massive amount of meat for our deep freeze, and I was then faced with the problem of how to prepare all this food. Thus began my experimentation in the kitchen – a first for me. In New York, I never cooked and had no clue where to start. I racked up a large phone bill calling Mom for recipes and help. I soon found that I thoroughly enjoyed the challenges of the kitchen and was able to teach Louie a lot of what I learned. Fortunately, Dave was very game and patient during my learning curve.

The only TV channel with any reception at that time in our house was ZBC, the government operated station, which was good only for a weather report. At eight o'clock each night, Dave would religiously watch a rudimentary forecast through a snowy screen and that was the extent of prime-time TV. Some people in the district had satellite TV and would videotape movies to pass around to friends. Gill Moolman, a neighbor, was very good about bringing us tapes to watch, but I truly enjoyed the time we shared without distraction. I generally sent the staff home by six o'clock, so that the evenings were private time. There is no doubt that a lack of television promotes a healthy sex life! We eventually had the satellite TV installed, and were able to enjoy modern entertainment – CNN, BBC, several sports stations and movie channels kept us up to date.

Our relationship was growing stronger everyday, and we were as at home with each other as ever. I learned quickly the true extent of Dave's understanding nature when, at random times, I would burst into tears with no explanation. I think the enormity of the move I had made, and the huge culture change I was experiencing sometimes overwhelmed me, without my even knowing it. I would cry uncontrollably in his arms, at the same time assuring him that I truly was very happy, while he gently wiped my tears.

Chapter 2

On my first Thursday, Dave told me there was no way we could escape going to the club that night. Thursday nights at the club were the big weekly gathering for Tengwe. I had heard him talk about it and was eager to meet his friends, but obviously I was nervous as well. We arrived at the club that night around seven. It was a very modest, one-story brick building with four tennis courts, a squash court, and a nine-hole golf course. A playground and trampoline for the children, a "kid's room," a large kitchen, a main hall, a stage and, most importantly, a bar were the center of activity. The side of the building that looked onto the tennis courts was windowed all the way, but once again, burglar bars blocked the view. Most, but not all, of the windows had thin, homemade curtains. There were old photographs of golfers, tennis players, fishing champions, cricket teams and squash teams on the walls behind the bar, and large plaques documenting each year's club champion. The common cement flooring extended throughout the rooms and kitchen.

I was immediately surrounded by a group of girls who whisked me off to their table. That night I met Gill and Meyer Moolman, Debbie and Leith Bray, Sharon and Andy Kockott, Serena Mason (wife of Pete), Jeff and

Barbs Kockott (our neighbors on one side), and many more. Gill was a petite blond who made it clear that she would be my caretaker for the night, and made me feel right at home. Debbie was an attractive, tall blond who was pregnant at the time and was very curious of how I came to be in Tengwe. Serena was a more reserved, classy brunette whose soft-spoken accent sounded very proper, but I found her to be as laid back as they come. Sharon Kockott intrigued me immediately, as she impressed me as a true African bush lady who was more comfortable in a natural setting. I am not sure how many times I actually saw her wearing shoes, but it did not nearly equal the number of times she was without them. I suddenly felt self-conscience in my body-suit, mini-skirt and clicky heels.

Despite the fact I was on display that night, I felt oddly at home among these strangers. It was a festive crowd of all ages, with numerous children running around on the playground outside. I learned that on Thursday and Saturday afternoons, the golfers would arrive for nine holes, and the tennis players would arrive for a match. There were no set matches, just whoever arrived would divide into groups and hit the course. After playing, they would come in and shower, or not, and join the others in the bar for drinks and dinner. The club was run entirely by the community. There was a permanent staff to maintain the grounds and the kitchen, but all the organization was done by the club committee members. A rotating roster appointed two members each week to be on bar duty, which meant the husbands would serve drinks while the wives organized supper on designated club nights. All members in the district were expected to do their bit for the club, as everyone enjoyed the social benefits the club provided. It was all very casual and easy-going, a refreshing contrast to the clubs I had known before.

I tried desperately to understand everything that was being said that night, but the lingo used in Zimbabwe is a unique one, and I struggled at first to pick up on the humor and the slang. The official language is English, but in reality, everyone I came across used a combination of English, Shona (the native language) and Afrikaans (a form of Dutch), usually all in one sentence. Not only is the lingo unique, it is also infectious. As soon as I learned the words and how to use them, I entered them into my own vocabulary. Some of their words and sayings just seemed to make more sense sometimes. One of my favorite sayings I could not live without is the use of the verb "to sort." It can be used to mean "fix," "arrange," "take care of," "set up" or anything related to these words. I came to understand that "Just the other day" could mean last week or last year, "Just down the road" could mean five miles or fifty miles away, and that "just now" could refer to immediate past or immediate future. Eventually, I found it much easier to be understood when I used the local lingo, although my distinct southern accent stood out like a sore thumb as I heard myself talking among the Zimbabweans! My staff was constantly amused by my attempts at Shona, mixed in with a few "ya'lls" here and there.

After dinner was served and the sun went down, I noticed several of the ladies retrieving their children from wherever they were playing, taking them outside. Upon returning to the bar without them, I was quite confused and Gill explained it was common practice for the kids to sleep in the backs of their trucks in the parking lot. Most farmers have a covered truck, either a double or single cab style, and mattresses were made to fit in the bed. Pillows, blankets, teddys and dolls were all thrown in on club nights, and the children were put to bed while the parents enjoyed themselves inside. Nannies were brought along on these nights as well in the cases where "littlies," or infants, were involved. I was so taken aback at first but came to understand that this worked for everyone. Babysitters are not common in Zimbabwe, as no one wanted to leave the children at home alone. Besides, the club nights were as fun for the children as they were for the adults.

Parents would periodically walk outside to check on the sleeping children and could report back if any child other than their own needed tending.

One of my funniest memories of meeting the people of Tengwe that first time at the club involves a man named Michael Mason. He was quite the card and decided he would show off for me a little. He said, "Ann, have you ever seen a flaming asshole?" I played along, replying no, and he proceeded to light a shot glass of Sambuca, pulled his shorts down slightly and went to put the fire out on his behind, a trick that should ideally suction the glass to the flesh without burning it, and thus putting the fire out. Michael had had a bit too much to drink leading up to his trick and failed to get the glass squarely on his bottom. He subsequently burnt a distinct ring on his "bum," sending the entire bar into fits of laughter and Michael hopping around the room, trying to remove the half-stuck, flaming glass. He has that scar still!

I left the club that night struck by the genuine kindness and unconditional welcome I had received. I already had been invited for tea and a dinner party the following week, and had agreed to join an exercise group who met twice a week. Dave and I were to leave the next day to spend our first weekend together back at Chisamba Camp in Lions Den where we had met.

Chapter 3

Our trip that weekend was my first "bush catering" experience, and I am quite sure I failed. I had no clue how to prepare for provisions required in the wild, all the way from meat to tin foil to toilet paper. Pete Fick joined us for the weekend, and we had a lot of fun reliving memories of the safari, as well as shooting some of the birds we had left behind in August.

The first night there I woke in the middle of the night, burning and itching terribly all over my back, stomach and neck. I realized Dave was also awake, also scratching. Only after he turned on his flashlight did we find the furry little caterpillar lying in our bed. Dave explained that these caterpillars could be very bothersome, as I was increasingly finding out. I rifled through my make-up bag to find anything to help, and we resorted to putting "Sea Breeze" antiseptic wash on ourselves, which eased the itching only slightly. We sat in bed that night, trying desperately not to scratch, and distracted ourselves by taking turns telling stories from our pasts. The discomfort eased after about an hour, and we could laugh about it the next day, but I was prompted to give my products-bag a complete makeover to arm us for any future insect attacks!

Dave lived up to his promise to take me to the Kariba house the next weekend. His parents had a lovely two-story house on the lake near the northern tip of the dam. Located in a development with other vacation homes, the house overlooked the Charara River, separated by a grassy plain full of acacia trees. The upstairs of the house was a large, dorm-like room with an open veranda, where we sorted out our bed, complete with a secure mosquito net. (Kariba is possibly one of the most malaria-ridden places in Zimbabwe, and we were on weekly prophylactic medication during the entire rainy season) Dave told me this was unquestionably the best room in the house. That night I understood why.

Being mid-December, it was extremely hot and the rainy season had just begun. The intense heat of the day brought fantastic thunderstorms that rolled over the hills across the lake, and we lay in our bed and watched the spectacular lightshow only nature can present, complete with jagged streaks of lightning and deafening crashes of thunder. After the rain, I was puzzled by a scrunching noise close by, and Dave pointed out a hungry hippo in the yard below the veranda, "cutting the grass." We fell asleep to the sound of cracking branches as elephants passed through the trees in front of the house.

With that rain, one of the first significant downpours of the rainy season, came the onslaught of "flying ants." Dave explained that these winged termites pour out of their colonies in the anthills at an excessive rate in order to frantically search for mates and reproduce. The initial rains bring out the largest quantities of flying ants, having waited all year to burst forth. This also coincides with the main breeding season for most of the birdlife, and these ants are a major staple in the diet of new chicks. As equally important, these ants are also considered some of the best fishing bait around, and I then understood what the tubs of ants were doing in the deep freeze. All predators from lions to mice benefit from this source of protein. The natives also collect them, smoke them over a fire, and eat them like snacks.

The next morning we went out on the boat, mainly for joy-riding, but some fishing as well. Dave drove us into the deep water of the lake where we could take a quick swim, safe from the hippos and crocodiles. There is a place in the lake called the gorge, a beautiful river valley surrounded by tall cliffs on either side that is legendary for fabulous fishing. We may have caught fish, but what I remember most is the secluded bay we pulled into for lunch. I had packed leftover "borewors" (a delicious spicy sausage), slices of cheddar cheese, crackers and boiled eggs (I obviously had not found my catering legs yet!) We drank Bohlinger beer, made love, and ate lunch naked on the boat, all the while surrounded by trees full of curious monkeys.

It had been two weeks since I had arrived back in Africa, and on that day I knew in my heart that I would marry Dave Beattie.

Chapter 4

The Christmas season was in full gear as we returned from Kariba, and I was to learn about the responsibilities of managing a staff 150 strong. On the farm, as on many farms, Dave and Andy ran a store. Ours was called "Katengwe Store" and Gill Moolman had been managing it for him. This job involved keeping it stocked, keeping track of credit accounts (deducted from monthly wages) and doing all the book-keeping. Dave's employees could buy all the basics – bread, meal, cooking oil, sugar, shampoo, soap, shoes, baby clothes, etc. – and run a monthly charge account of sorts. The store was open to the public as well, but not for credit purchases. A woman living on the neighboring farm, named Spiwe, was the store-keeper who ran the day-to-day operations. Managing the store was to become my job eventually, but that Christmas I was still struggling to find my way around the farm and drive on the right-hand side of the car and the left-hand side of the road. In rural areas like Tengwe, the main roads have a "narrow tar" system, which is a single paved lane in the middle of a dirt road. When two cars come from opposite directions, each pulls off the road so that the outside tire is on the dirt. After passing safely by, the cars go back onto the tar. Of course, my instinct was to pull off to the right side, when really I needed to be on the left. Most of Tengwe began to recognize that I was driving and gave me a wide berth!

Every year at Christmas, Dave and Andy slaughtered a cow, ordered kegs of beer, and gave out candy and bonuses to the workers and their families. The community of the workforce was like an extended family, and Dave and Andy were always very generous on many levels. One day near Christmas, Dave asked me to go to the store and get some bags of candy for the kids on the farm. I was so distraught because I did not know how to get to the store and was too embarrassed to tell Dave, but finally had to confess to my ignorance because he couldn't understand the problem. Zimbabweans have a knack for giving directions like, "Turn right at the fig tree and go until there is a break in the contour and turn left." Another common baffling instruction is "Follow your nose." Coming from New York City, I really didn't see too many fig trees or contours in tobacco fields!

In reality, the store was about three quarters of a mile from my house, a walk I came to do regularly. Eventually, I did learn to run the store efficiently, and I actually learned to drive on the left side of the road. I had been a confident and sometimes cocky New Yorker, but learned quickly how humbling it can be outside of one's element. Not much of what I learned in New York or Chapel Hill could be applied to rural Africa, and I had to dig deep within myself to find the confidence and stamina to learn and adapt to a whole new way of life.

One day at our house, having tea with Shirley and Andy, I was petting Bella and felt a big lump on her skin. I said to Dave, "I think Bella has a big tick." He felt it and said "No, not a tick." Upon closer inspection, we found many lumps like it all over her body. He said, "She has putsies." I said, "What's that?" Turns out "putsy" is a cute word for maggot. The maggot fly lays an egg on some vulnerable soft spot like puppy or baby or human skin, and then grows into a worm, which hatches out of the skin when it is ready.

Dave got some medicine used on the cattle to treat ticks (ironically called "Exit") and sprayed it on the lumps. After about ten seconds, a white worm would wiggle its way out of Bella's skin, leaving a hole about a quarter inch in diameter. We would squash the worm and spray the next lump. We must have extracted about fifty maggots that day. I was sick to my stomach, but at the same time fascinated by this process of nature. After I related this incident to my friend, Serena, she told me that yes, putsies are a problem, and her first-born, Lindsay, had an encounter as a baby. She had about one hundred putsies in her head at one year old! I was horrified. And that is why all items of clothing and linen had to be ironed when brought in from the clothesline – the maggots lay eggs in damp places and the heat of the iron kills them.

I had finally worked up the confidence to walk with the dogs around the farm everyday, a pleasure for me as much as for them. As soon as I walked out with my tennis-shoes and walkman, the dogs would go wild, knowing we were venturing out. One day, Sam was in heat and Dave recommended I not take her, but I did not have the heart to leave her behind. I was about a mile from the house when I noticed the dogs behaving oddly. I looked behind me to find a jackal (a type of wild dog) trotting steadily towards me. I walked faster, and so did he. I began to jog, and so did he. Then I began to run, and so did he. My heart was racing and I had no idea what this creature could do to me – it wasn't very big – and I ran faster. The dogs kept my pace even more so, and by the time I turned onto another road, the jackal had lost interest. I continued to run until I got home and called Dave on the radio, forgetting that his parents could also hear me. I was frantic in my story, but what I didn't know was that dogs in heat attract interest from any animal within several miles, so it was the dog the jackal was interested in, not me. At that time, Dave, Andy and Shirley collectively decided that I would not walk without a radio slung on my shorts so I could call if I ever had another episode. I felt a little foolish, needless to say.

Chapter 5

Christmas that year was nothing less than bizarre for me. Never in my life had I imagined spending Christmas day in my bathing suit – swimming costume, shortened to "cossie" in Zimbabwe. It was a Beattie family tradition to pack Christmas and take it all up to Kariba, and that year was no different.

Dave and I had driven to Harare, a two and a half hour drive, to pick up his daughter, Kim, age five, from her mother, Susie. Obviously, this was a nervous time for me. I had met Susie's parents, as they lived in Tengwe, but had not yet met his ex-wife or his daughter. Kimi was quiet on the ride to the farm, and I could see she was unsure of my presence, but curious of my accent and my words. During the few days we had at home before heading to the lake, we were able to break the barrier. She began imitating some of my pronunciations, like "plant," and was so amused by my attempts at "chongololo," the Shona word for millipede, which I obviously said like a true southerner! At first, I was shocked to find these black, hard-shelled, humongous worm-like creatures in the house constantly. Over time, instead of calling for Louie or Irene to evacuate them, I began to kick them out like everyone else. I learned that if I tapped them first with my toe, they would coil up in protection, and it was easier to kick them in that shape.

Dave's older sister and her family, Cheryl and Dean Barnes, who live in South Africa, had driven up for Christmas with their children, Leigh and Joelle, who were twelve and nine. It was a festive gathering of cousins and siblings at Kariba. I was the newcomer, and had much to learn about family Christmas traditions, but felt right at home all the same. We caught fish, went for booze cruises every evening, decorated an indigenous tree cut from the bush, and spent many hours in the pool.

On Christmas day, after all the "pressies" were opened, I could see Dave was a little fidgety, and wondered why he didn't want to go fishing. I then learned the golden rule of the Beattie family – NO FISHING ON CHRISTMAS DAY. This was set in place many years before by Andy's mother, and was abided by still. I had scored big with Kimi by bringing the latest Barbie doll from FAO Schwartz, and we were starting to bond nicely. She had been eyeing my make-up bag for some days, and when I finally gave her access, she "made-up" Dave, complete with lipstick and eyeshadow, much to her delight!

Dave gave me a stereo that first Christmas, something we needed and wanted desperately in the house, but it became a bit of a joke between us as it was such an unusual gift to give so early in a relationship. I used to joke, "Wonder if my stereo will fit the plug in New York?" and Dave would say "I don't know – I wonder," but we both knew that stereo was going nowhere but Tengwe.

As New Year's Eve approached, Dave and I drove back to Tengwe to join in the annual festivities at the club. I had been told that New Year's Eve was the biggest "do" of the year with much preparation. The crowd was usually about two hundred people, with music of some kind and a three course dinner. The day of the party, Dave and I went up to the club to help out and found the men all busy raising a large tent outside, some women bustling in the kitchen, preparing an extensive menu, and some in the hall putting up decorations. I was overwhelmed by the scene and didn't really know how to help at first, but was soon given a job in the kitchen. If someone had told me on that day that the "Entertainment Committee" at the club was to become my baby, I would have felt very sorry for the club. As I have said, I learned a lot.

The party was absolutely one of the most festive I have known. Almost the entire community arrived, dressed to the nines, and ready for a party. Tradition held that dinner was to be served around nine o'clock, then dancing and nonsense ensued until the sun came up. At sunrise, the cricket bats and balls were brought out, and while breakfast was prepared, whoever was left standing divided into teams for a game of cricket. This was usually quite funny to watch, as there were some pretty unsteady legs out there! As normal, the parking lot was full of sleeping children who had spent a peaceful night while their parents had a ball.

Near the end of the holidays, Dave took me to Kadoma, a town in the Midlands where his greatest childhood friend, Douglas Kok, lived. I had heard many stories of this colorful character, and was anxious to meet him. I am sure I will never be greeted in the same way ever again, for when I walked up to shake his hand, he hugged me and said indirectly to Dave, "Well done, Beattie! She's got good breeding hips!" I was so taken aback, not to mention self-conscious of my hippiness, I did not know how to react to this one. As a true man of the bush, I came to know that Douglas sees most things through the eyes of a professional hunter, sizing up species on specific physical merits. Douglas entertained us that night, as he has done many nights now, with stories from the wild, and he and Dave enjoyed reliving their childhood memories by telling me tales of shooting birds out of Shirley's trees when she wasn't looking, drinking a case of cokes in one night, or cooking their first duiker over a fire in the woods.

The holidays came to a close and that year was a big one for Kimi, as she was to begin boarding school in January. At the tender age of five, she went to school in Marondera, about an hour from her house, and four hours from Tengwe, where she spent Monday through Friday. This concept is something that all farm children in Zimbabwe are accustomed to, and the school system was a very strong, disciplined, English curriculum. Weekends at home were cherished time, devoted wholly to play and fun, while the dorm-mothers and teachers took care of the education and homework during the week. The kids adjusted to the routine a little better than most of the mothers did! There was some comfort in knowing that any older siblings or friends from the district always looked after the little ones.

It was a particularly difficult time for Dave, as Kimi's start of school meant less time with him, as he then had to settle for long weekends every third weekend as the distance was so great. All the same, he made the long drive any chance he could to bring her home, and we continued to grow closer that summer.

The rainy season was in full swing, and as important as it was, too much rain could also be a problem. The rainy season basically runs from mid-November through March/ April. The Intertropical Convergence Zone (ITCZ) is crucial to the rain patterns of Southern Africa and is a topic much discussed at any social event. I could go for days without walking the dogs, simply because the dirt roads of the farm were impassable in some spots. I was frustrated that I did not have much independence at that point and was pretty much reliant on Dave, his parents or a friend to take me somewhere. It took a while to gain the confidence to drive to Karoi and Harare on my own, but eventually I overcame my doubts and fears and gained more autonomy. It seems so simple, but driving on the opposite side of the road and car can be very intimidating, and instinct could not be trusted. Inconsistent is a polite term to describe the party-line telephone system of that day, and it really could not be relied on for much, so chats with girlfriends were difficult at best. The most effective way to talk to someone was to pop in for tea.

I became accustomed to the daily routine of the farm. Our days began at sunrise, Dave would return around eight o'clock for breakfast, and then would be back in the lands or at the workshops until lunch at noon, but he always stopped for tea, either at his Mom's or at home. During the mornings, I would either go for a walk, go to Karoi for shopping and errands, work in the garden, or busy myself with projects around the house.

One time I needed to go shopping in Karoi and Gill offered to take me. She had told me about "The Shed" in Karoi, and I was curious to see the place many ladies went to buy clothes. I had complimented her new Calvin Klein jeans one day, wondering where she could have bought them, and she told me she found them at The Shed for a ridiculously small amount of money. The scene inside was astounding – stacks and stacks of clothes piled on tables, and hundreds of African women and even some "Euros" (whites) pouring through piles of second-hand clothing. This would be deemed one of those places where "you really have to look" in order to find something. I was stunned to realize that this place, affectionately called "Little Harrods," was selling the donated clothes from the aid agencies in other countries! It did not exactly appeal to me, especially when I observed a woman change her baby's dirty nappy on top of one of the piles.

Depending on the day, someone would inevitably stop in for tea, as our house was very centrally located within Tengwe. These impromptu visits always kept us in the know with what was going on around the community! After lunch, we had a kip until two o'clock, during which time it was unheard of to call or radio someone during these hours on a farm. The staff would all go home as well. I must admit, during the early years of our relationship, Dave and I did not do too much resting at rest-time! At two, Dave would go back to work until tea at four or so, and then the workday was pretty much done. A tradition I came to love was "potluck" dinners. More often than not, a friend would radio in the afternoon and say "Come around this evening for potluck," meaning no fancy dinner, just whatever is in the fridge. These nights could end up being some of our best parties! Trips to Harare came every week or so and were a welcome change to the routine, but a day or two in the city usually left us haggard and ready to go home.

That growing and curing season, I learned much about tobacco farming. Dave took me for rides on the motorbike almost everyday and explained all the stages of the process. His meticulous and instinctive farming methods always paid off. He was extremely disciplined about checking the barns at all hours during the curing process, a very crucial step as temperatures had to be maintained by adding coal to the fire in order to cure the leaves perfectly. Woe to any barn attendant who was found sleeping on the job (even at three in the morning!). I loved the distinctive, musky smell of curing tobacco Dave carried with him when he came home from the barns. It was fascinating to watch the women in the grading shed tie the perfectly cured, pliable yellow leaves into "hands," groups of five leaves, to be packaged for auction.

During those months, I also discovered much about establishing a garden. Dave had traded Clever in for Never, a more experienced and capable garden boy who thankfully spoke more English. The names of the employees were an endless source of amusement for me. The roster on our farm included names like Mattress, Smart, Brain, Lovemore, Getmore, Toomuch and Toomany. Dave explained that from the early days of colonial rule, African workers with names unpronounceable to the British settlers began giving themselves work names in order to facilitate communication. Over time, the parents began giving an English name to children at birth. The last name always remained the Shona name and never changed. Robert Mugabe is a perfect example of this.

Never was very eager to help me arrange a beautiful garden, and fortunately I had skilled and knowledgeable friends who guided me, for I had no experience growing anything in a sub-tropical climate, or any climate, for that matter. I gradually came to appreciate the challenge and satisfaction a garden can provide, something that had never held my attention before.

As happy as I was in my newly acquired lifestyle, there were certainly times during those first months that I felt alienated and somewhat lonesome, but I have always been one to cherish my time alone. It was unusual to wake in the mornings with no job or immediate responsibility. I didn't have history with these people, and there were always the "remember when" stories that left me feeling like I was from some other planet. I knew that patience and time would change all these things, and so when considering my future, I did not doubt that Tengwe could be my home. There was no question as to whether or not Dave and I belonged together. It was just a matter of making it permanent.

It had been our plan from the beginning that I would stay for a maximum of five months on that first visit. I was already committed to participating in three weddings that spring and summer in the States and had no choice but to be back for them. Mid-April was our deadline, and as February ended, April didn't seem too far off. We decided that Dave would accompany me back to the States that spring, so that he could meet my friends and see my family. At the time of booking his plane ticket, we also booked another one for my return in July. This was cause for many questions and speculation, but we were pretty quiet about our plans.

Before our departure, some friends gave us a send-off unlike any other. Andy and Sharon Kockott had a farm down the road from us which had a large, beautiful dam, one of our favorite spots in Tengwe, aptly named Tengwe Dam. Dams in Zimbabwe are the equivalent to our ponds or lakes, not our actual dams. Sharon organized a three course dinner, complete with silver goblets and china, on their pontoon boat where she had laid a beautiful dining table, and invited our good friends Gill and Meyer Moolman. The Indian influence throughout Southern Africa is a strong one, and curry is a traditional and popular dish, served with a variety of sambals, condiments that complement the spicy dish such as tomato, onion, cucumber, banana, peanuts, coconut and chutney. Pappadums must be served on the side. The six of us floated on the dam and had an exquisite meal of lamb curry, and lots of wine and laughs until late in the evening.

Dave and I landed in the States in April, where Mom met us and could hardly contain her excitement and curiosity.

Chapter 6

Mom did not let too much time pass before she cornered Dave at dinner that first night with "Just what are your intentions with my daughter?" He was quite taken aback – brazen forwardness was not the Zimbabwean way – but handled her with his usual grace and dignity, as he assured her that we would indeed be married. I think it was our living together that bothered her most.

Our trip that spring was filled with wedding parties in the true southern style. Dave was amazed at the way a wedding celebration could be stretched over four days. We managed to squeeze in a visit to New York, a quick trip where I was able to introduce him to the real New York I knew, not the Times Square experience he had encountered on his one and only previous trip. We flew out to San Francisco to see the Corpening twins, and we spent some time at the beach in North Carolina. By the end of Dave's stay, he had probably met every friend I had and had charmed them all. He flew home the first week of June, and I was to follow at the end of July. I was absolutely miserable as I put him on the plane. All I wanted was to go with him. I had seven weeks to kill in High Point, and it turned out to be the longest seven weeks of my life.

My mother swears I was awful to live with and that I moped around like a spoiled brat. My oldest and best friend from childhood, Anne Wilson, was getting married in July and I was the maid-of-honor in her wedding. She knows me well and also detected my antsy behavior, but she was, as always, a steadfast and supportive friend, pleased for me and my newfound happiness. Mom and I attended a luncheon in her honor, and accompanied her to the bridal shop for her final dress fitting afterwards. I found the exact dress I wanted to be married in while waiting for Anne to try hers on. The simple and elegant sleeveless dress with a flared bottom was the perfect look I wanted for the outdoor wedding I fantasized about. Mom bought it on the spot, along with a large wide brim hat which actually cost more than the dress. The ladies in the bridal shop were a little confused when they saw no ring on my finger, and I could not give them an actual wedding date. Because I knew I would not find a dress like that in Zimbabwe, it only made sense to go ahead and get it.

My departure date finally arrived, and I was more than ready to get back to Dave. Mom and Aubrey were coming to the farm that August, so there were no teary goodbyes. After spending a torturous amount of time away from the man I loved, I knew once and for all that I was truly returning to the only place I wanted to call home.

PART THREE

TENGWE

Chapter 1

Upon my arrival in Tengwe, I was met with a round of welcome home parties and felt so complete within myself to be back with Dave, as well as with our friends. As it was the middle of the tobacco selling season, there was not much work going on around the farm, and we were busy preparing for Mom and Aubrey's arrival the first week of August. Aubrey was to be with us for two weeks, and Mom was staying on for a month. My good friend from New York, Carol Buckner, was to join us for the latter two weeks of Mom's stay. Mom had met Carol on her trip to Kenya and became fast friends, and she subsequently became a good friend of mine as well.

In preparation for their arrival, Dave set up several bird shoots around Tengwe and Karoi. All keen bird-shooters grew fields of sunflowers to ensure a healthy crop of doves, and that year was no exception. During their stay, we traveled up to Nyanga, a mountainous region located near the Mozambique border in the Eastern highlands of Zimbabwe. We were able to enjoy crisp mountain weather and successful trout fishing in the prolific dams and streams. I was eager to share the Kariba experience with them, and during our stay a herd of twenty elephants put on a fabulous show in front of the house for my family! We took them to a tobacco sale which is quite a site to behold, if you can withstand the intense level of nicotine on the auction floor. Rows and rows of heavy tobacco bales were wheeled onto the large floor, while auctioneers auctioned each bale to a line of buying reps from various tobacco companies from around the world. The selling farmer was always lurking behind, nervously watching the price.

Aubrey thoroughly enjoyed being on the farm and having the convenience of walking out the door with Freckles, the old pointer, to shoot birds whenever he wanted. I was so proud to show off my new kitchen skills to Mom, as well as my new found love of gardening. With large yards and plentiful staff, it was a very pleasurable type of gardening. August and September (the spring months) arrived with their own colors; vibrant red flamboyant trees, purple jacarandas, yellow cassia trees, poppies and sweet peas all brightened the dusty days of the dry season. The contrast between the dry and rainy season is vast. The wet months are typical of any summer – lush green grass, trees, and fauna surrounds the landscape under puffy thunderheads. In the dry months of winter and spring, except for private gardens with water supplies, the countryside takes on a harsh, barren look, but never loses its stark beauty.

My friends in Tengwe were as welcoming to my family as they were to me, and Mom and Aubrey were immediately struck by their warmness, as I had been months earlier. Some of the older ladies invited Mom on several golfing outings and my friends entertained my family in true Tengwe style. Cloudless, clear days provide the stunning sunsets Africa is famous for, the consolidated sources of food and water in the winter make for excellent bird shooting, and the impossibility of rain conveniently accommodates outdoor entertaining. Sunday lunches were a common source of fun for us, and often lasted through dinner, though Dave attended these social events grudgingly as it cut into his fishing time. The cool nights and mornings of June, July and August give way to warm days, and by September, summer temperatures creep back by mid-month. If we had more than one frost on the farm, it was a lot, and that was the extent of our winter. At first I couldn't believe how sensitive all the Tengwe-ites were to their "cold" weather, and poked fun when they would claim, "It's freezing!" at sixty degrees. In the end, I became so acclimated to the climate of Zimbabwe, that I still find sixty degrees way too chilly. There was no need for temperature control beyond fans and space heaters on the farm, though Kariba is a different story with its sultry and oppressive heat in mid-summer.

I had brought back some gourmet greens seed, a trend that had not caught on in Zimbabwe yet (they were still into iceberg lettuce) and was thrilled to fill my vegetable garden with colorful, leafy greens. I introduced the tasty leaves to my friends and they just went wild. I planted loads of yellow crookneck squash, a vegetable unknown to Zimbabwe, and introduced Tex-Mex foods like tacos, chili and nachos to them as well. Debbie remarked once that eating at the Beattie's was like going to another country! Of course, I had my share of learning to do about new foods. Youngberry bushes, litchie, guava, pawpaw, mango and grapefruit trees filled a whole section of my yard. Thankfully, Shirley was very skilled in making jams and marmalade, and I would have Never pick the ripe fruits and take them to her house for preparation. I learned how to deal with foods in bulk, for people were constantly passing along excess fruits and vegetables, depending on what was in season. Some could be frozen, some had to be stewed and then frozen, some I made into soups, and some I just gave to the staff if there was too much. The luxury of having freshly picked fruits and vegetables at our easy disposal is something I came to take for granted. It was just too easy to tell Louie I needed two cups of fresh lemon juice and then have it almost instantly. When I first arrived in Tengwe, I noticed after a couple of weeks that milk somehow magically appeared in my refrigerator every few days. When I asked Dave about its source, he explained that our neighbors Jeff and Barbs Kockott had dairy cows. They had been kind to Dave during his bachelor days and sent one of their cattle boys over periodically with some fresh farm milk. This was thick, fresh and not pastuerized, a taste I had to get used to. It was such a luxury to have it delivered, but we decided they really did not need to provide us with milk anymore, as there was now a lady in the house.

Dave and I intended to be engaged by the time Mom and Aubrey left, but our plan was a little sketchy on details. I had learned by that time that Dave had mastered the art of procrastination, and I did not want to seem too pushy about getting a ring on my finger, but Aubrey's time with us was drawing to a close and there was still no engagement. Two days before Aubrey was to fly out, Dave had to go to Harare for a tobacco sale and a dental appointment. He was very late getting home and got out of the car with a huge scowl on his face. As it turned out, the poor man had ended up getting a root-canal, something he wasn't expecting. Considering his mood, I was not about to ask him whether he managed to pick up a diamond along the way!

As we dressed to go to Shirley and Andy's house for a send-off dinner for Aub, Dave surprised me with the emerald and diamond ring I had admired some weeks before. We had a happy, festive family celebration that night and decided the wedding would be that December, an easy time of year for Mom and Aubrey to make a return trip. I did not think twice about getting married in Zimbabwe; I had embraced the community as my new home and wanted to get married there. We booked the Bosmans' camp in Lions Den where we had started our romance and set our wedding date for December 28, 1996.

Carol arrived that next day as we put Aubrey on the plane. Mom,

Carol and I drove (for the first time by myself!) to the camp in Lions Den to scope out tent sites and table placements for the wedding. I truly was on such a high; I cannot remember a time in my life when I have ever been more fulfilled and content. During this time, I threw my first party of any substance for Dave's birthday and had such fun cooking and decorating, and of course, partying, that it became an annual event at my house on August 25th. Without the deterrent of cleaning up, entertaining large crowds was relatively easy. I learned that if I did not come out of my room until eight o'clock the next morning, all signs of the previous nights' revelry would magically disappear! My staff grew accustomed to my penchant for throwing parties over the years and were always rewarded with leftovers the next day.

When Mom and Carol's trip came to a close, we went to Harare for the night in order to do some shopping before they got on the plane. I took them to the shopping center in Borrowdale, a wealthy suburb of Harare, to show them that true shopping did exist in Zimbabwe. Carol's comment to me was "I feel so much better about where you are now that I see this!" So many of my friends from the U.S. really had no idea what kind of environment I was living in, and most pictured rustic tents in the wild bush. I encouraged them to visit us so that they could understand a little more of what real life was like for me in Africa.

After Mom and Carol left, I was faced with the daunting task of planning my wedding. I was extremely lucky to have so many friends who knew the ropes. Debbie Bray and I spent two days in Harare sorting out the caterers. I was a little skeptical of how it was all going to come together in a remote site with no electricity, two hours from Harare. The two men in charge assured me that they had done this many times, and we went on to set the menu for an exquisite three-course meal. My friend Sharon Kockott was placed in charge of flowers, and I challenged her by requesting blue hydrangeas, my very favorite but a hard-to-find flower in Zimbabwe. I met with the rental company, and they also assured me that they could find the unmarked dirt roads that led to the secluded camp in Lions Den to deliver the tents, tables, china and glassware. I spent many hours pouring through old rain records to see how many times in the last fifteen years it had rained on December 28, and the odds were not in my favor.

The wedding plans were progressing well as November rolled around. Some old friends of Dave's, Jamie and Mandy Saul, had recently moved to Tengwe to lease a tobacco farm. One Thursday afternoon, Mandy and I went up to the club for tennis while Dave and Jamie went fishing. As the sun went down, Mandy persuaded me to play one more set. As I back-pedaled to return a lob, I lost my footing, fell backwards, caught myself with my left hand, and broke my wrist so completely that my hand was at a ninety degree angle with my arm. Everyone on the court heard the snap, and I was in shock. I stared at my disfigured wrist while someone tried to fix me a sling, someone else radioed Dave, and someone else called the doctor in Chinhoyi to alert him I would be coming. I fell into a deeper state of shock as I realized what was ahead of me – the closest doctor was a ninety minute drive away, and my wrist began to throb painfully. Gill must have seen me fading because she slapped my face, which actually did wake me up and gave everyone else such a laugh that it broke the tension. Dave arrived and we took off on the bumpiest, longest ride I have known. I tried to keep my arm braced against my chest so that every bump in the road didn't hurt so much, but it was a pretty futile act as the roads were full of potholes in many areas. Finally, we arrived at the doctors' office where Dr. Stilgoe was waiting for us. He immediately gave me a shot for pain, x-rayed my arm and then put me to sleep while he set my wrist. When I woke up, I was in a soft cast, and Dave and Gill were waiting for me. There were two doctors in Chinhoyi who were on call for everything from a broken wrist to a snake bite to a heart-attack, and I do believe they had seen it all.

All I could think about, aside from the agonizing throbbing of my wrist, was my wedding. I desperately did not want a cast on my arm for that day and hoped it would be off by then.

Chapter 2

Fortunately, my cast did come off in time for Mom and Aubrey's arrival for a family Christmas that year on the farm. We decided to postpone the Kariba trip until after the wedding, as there was so much going on. We had a memorable family Christmas that year with all of my family as well as all of Dave's family. Kimi joined us on Boxing Day and we were in full wedding mode, tending to last minute details. Interestingly, Mom and I had agreed that Dave and I would organize and pay for all the wedding activities, and she would reimburse us in US dollars in our account in the States. At the time of our wedding, the exchange rate was ten Zimbabwe dollars to one US dollar. Tourists loved it because foreign money had so much buying power in Zimbabwe. Mom got away with a seven thousand U.S. dollar wedding without cutting any corners.

Our minister, Rob Haarhoff, was a man we had gotten to know very well. He gave an Anglican service every third Sunday at the Tengwe Church and was an avid fisherman when he had the time. He and Dave bonded on the water as much as anywhere, and he often stayed with us when he was in the district. It was very special to have a man we respected so much to perform our wedding.

It was on the day before the wedding that I truly realized the generous nature of the friends I had. Gill, Sharon, Serena, Debbie and Mandy were all at Lions Den to make sure everything was in place and set-up. Gill and

Sharon were waiting for the flowers to arrive. I had been forewarned that the hydrangeas would not be available, something I had prepared myself for, and the back-up plan was white roses. We set up the tables, the table cloths, the bar, the generator and everything else that could be arranged ahead of time. The dining lodge, an oval, brick, open thatched structure with trophies of every kind on the walls (kudu, bushbuck, buffalo, wildebeest, impala, sable to name a few), was the perfect size to hold the round tables for 110 guests, and the "kids tent" set up off to the side would accommodate almost the same number of children. A small tent off the lodge was erected for the ceremony which overlooked the large, scenic dam. By five that afternoon, we were all exhausted and ready to go home except that the flowers had not arrived yet. Sharon was trying to convince me to go home when a truck barreled into camp laden with boxes and boxes of blue hydrangeas. I was beside myself! She herself was not sure they would arrive and had not wanted to get my hopes up. A family friend Neil Purdon a man well-connected in the flower industry came through for us and absolutely made my day. Not only did he produce these elusive flowers, he **gave** them to us as our wedding present.

I woke on my wedding day very early, and Mom and I drove to Lions Den in order to dress for the noon event. Despite the flat tire Dave and Aubrey had on the way to the camp, everything was running smoothly until the caterers arrived and panicked when they realized there had been a misunderstanding as to who would provide chafing dishes, and there were none. All I could do was let my capable friends "make a plan," which, of course, they did with no problem by converting old camp kitchen trays into presentable serving platters. Aubrey walked me down the aisle on a pristine summer day that December, and Dave and I were wed before a group of our best friends and family.

I did not want that day to end. The kids had a blast running amok around the camp, and the adults had even more fun, dancing all afternoon to the fabulous music provided by my friend Heather, a DJ from Harare. Pete Mason, our emcee, kept the crowd laughing with his wit and humor, and Aubrey and Mom gave eloquent speeches. The rain shower that came at three that afternoon was well timed, as with farmers, rain only adds an excuse to celebrate even more. This usually involved dancing in the rain, and my gorgeous dress still has stains from the red mud common in Lions Den. Dave and I were scheduled to spend the night at Meikles Hotel in Harare, but we did not leave the party until eight o'clock as we were having too much fun. When we did finally pull ourselves away, the kids formed an archway out of fishing rods for us to walk through!

We enjoyed a relaxing week in the Comores for our honeymoon, an island nation off the coast of Madagascar, where we stayed at a lovely hotel that was an oasis among vast poverty, as is often the case in third world countries.

Chapter 3

Upon our return home, Dave went right into the curing season, the busiest time on the farm. We had by then taken over the cropping operations that season and were enthusiastic about being in business for ourselves. Our company was named Druswick Enterprises, and we ran it as partners.

I was in charge of all administrative work and payroll. Once a month, I sat down with Evans, the farm clerk who was Irene's brother, with piles of cash stacked in front of me, and counted out each person's monthly wage. Evans kept track of who worked how many days and gave me the books at the end of the month. I would enter all the information on the computer and calculate the figures on spreadsheets in Excel. In today's banking world, it would be deemed an archaic system, but believe me, I had computerized it as much as I possibly could. Most of our employees did not keep bank accounts and had to be paid in cash. We also had to figure in loan payments for those who had taken out loans from Dave during the month, as well as how much credit they had used at the store. I took a little from those who owed money, but it never made sense to deduct too much, for they would just be at the back door the next day, asking for another loan. Dave was usually understanding when his workers needed extra money to pay for schooling or medical expenses, but many times he refused loans to those he knew were blowing their money at the local pub in the township. On Katengwe Farm, we always knew when it was payday, for the first Saturday of the month would bring a loud party at that bar in the "location." Being situated so close to Tengwe itself, our house actually rocked to the beat of the drums that bands banged on all night on those occasions, even though we were a mile away.

In the farming business, as selling season runs only four to five months of the year from May to September, significant loans from banks were necessary to grow such large crops. Every October, we would negotiate with Standard Chartered Bank in order to secure a loan for the expensive resources necessary to see the crop through the growing season. The chemicals, fertilizers, coal, diesel and payroll required to produce high quality tobacco all came at a premium. I watched the overdraft grow and grow, as well as the interest, until the sales began in May. The overdraft would usually be paid off by the middle of the selling season, and the rest was ours, but I found it incredibly nerve-racking in the beginning to owe such large amounts of money and to be dependent on Mother Nature to ensure a good crop. Dave, an excellent farmer, always reassured me that we would be OK, and went on to be awarded as one of Tengwe's top growers every year we were in business. Each year, after we paid off the loan, we would exchange as much money as we could for US dollars and send it to our account in the States. Most people in Zimbabwe knew all too well the unstable political tendencies of Robert Mugabe, and while the scene was relatively quiet at that time in 1997, one could never be sure about the future of the currency. The black market for foreign exchange is a profitable business in most African nations, and Zimbabwe is no different. Exchanging large sums of money this way is illegal and could be dangerous, but it was always worth the risk. In my early years, US dollars were available through exchange companies, and each person was allowed to buy five thousand US dollars a year, which was marked in our passports. Any amounts over and above that had to be done on the sly. Eventually, those companies closed down because the foreign exchange became so scarce, available only on the black market.

That same season, Dave and I began to meet with architects to design the house we planned to build on a beautiful site on the Dendera farm dam, near Shirley and Andy's house. Our dream house was designed to take full advantage of the view overlooking Dendera dam, tucked privately in the woods, and catered to all our architectural whims. Arched doorways and windows, multiple verandas, tiled roofing, tiled flooring, spacious bedrooms and an upstairs master bedroom en suite all fit into our carefully executed house plan. Dave hired a brick-maker to come to the farm and build twice as many kilns that year as he usually did, in order to supply the materials for our house. Dendera and Katengwe farms had more than enough clay for brick-making, as there was a bountiful supply of anthills, or termite mounds, throughout the farms. These mounds were massive, cone-shaped clay structures made by the termites and could average a height of ten feet and diameter of anywhere up to sixty feet. Because the antbears, or aardvarks, would tunnel in after the termites, these mounds provided ideal housing for other animals such as warthogs, snakes, jackals and porcupines, to name a few. Enriched by the workings of the termites, they also afforded a healthy environment for many types of flora, mainly fig and fruit bearing trees, mahogany trees and euphorbia trees (a cactus-like tree which was Tengwe's own emblem). Many farmers cleared these anthills when preparing fields for crops, but Dave was adamant that none be destroyed, except when needed for bricks, because they more importantly served as satellite oases that provided protection and cover for the bird population from raptors that were common in our area, like falcons, eagles and hawks.

The brick making process fascinated me, mainly because I had never pondered the origin of a brick before, but also because it could all be done right there on the farm. The anthill clay, mixed with water, was put in a wooden mold and then turned out on to level ground to be sun-dried. The bricks would then be built into a large kiln, interspersed with coal, and set alight. The kiln burned for a week and each oven produced about 45,000 bricks.

As the reaping and curing season came to a close, we were busy planning a big trip to Mozambique in April with four other couples. The group totaled nineteen in all, ten adults and nine children. Dave and the Moolmans had been to this camp on the coast the year before and insisted we all experience the paradise they had found. We convoyed in five vehicles for a two-day drive through Zimbabwe, across the eastern border, into Mozambique, through a stunning rain forest, through several armed roadblocks, and finally down the escarpment to the pristine coast. In the town of Vilanculos, we unloaded our gear onto a dhow, a type of sailboat used to transport supplies, and we climbed into several ski boats to take us across to Pontamingo, a point where a tented camp was set up in the dunes. The dhow only arrived the next morning as it was subject to the changing tides. The tents in the camp could sleep a family of five comfortably, and each one had running water, showers, sinks and loos. Here we spent two of the finest weeks of our lives. We had the entire undeveloped beach to ourselves, the surf fishing was extraordinary, the water was crystal blue, and the sand was pure white and riddled with gigantic, gorgeous shells. The men used fourteen foot rods to catch fifty pound kingfish, pompano and queenfish right on the beach. We had brought all our food and drinks, packed in several coolers and trunks, but had to resort to Mozambiquean beer the last few days. We christened a new dance, called the Pontamingo Shuffle, that we did along the dunes sometimes heading back to our tents in the dark after late nights and many drinks at the bar!

We reluctantly packed up and headed home, dreading the long ride ahead. One of the vehicles had a flat tire, and we had been told that there was a little village on the way that could repair the tire. From what we had seen as we drove through, I wasn't too sure about that. Zimbabwe may have been third-world, but Mozambique was forth or fifth-world, having collapsed economically and politically after its independence from Portugal in the 1960's. We were amused at the exchange rate of the Zim dollar at that time of one to one thousand Mozambican meticais. As it turned out, the road took us through a cluster of buildings in the woods, a village called Sussendenga, where the Kockotts were indeed able to get their tire repaired!

In May, we headed up to Nyanga for the annual trout-fishing competition some of the Tengwe men participated in. The wives were included that year, and we stayed at the beautiful Rhodes Nyanga Hotel, named after Cecil Rhodes, who had founded Rhodesia. It was a social occasion with lots of friends around, but I was feeling a little out of sorts that weekend. On our way home, we stopped in Harare, where upon seeing the doctor, I confirmed my suspicions. I was pregnant. According to my calculations, my baby had been conceived in Mozambique, something that amused my friends to no end and they insisted we name the child Jose!

During that trip to Nyanga, I met Norma Saul, the matriarch of the large Saul family (mother to our friend Jamie), who was very close to Dave as he had spent a great deal of time at their farm during his childhood. She and her husband, Ronnie, had very strong Scottish accents and were difficult to understand at first, but I soon caught on to the rhythm of their speech. Norma asked me how I was adjusting to life in Africa, and as we discussed the differences of life on a farm, she told me a story of her own when she had landed on Ronnie's farm straight from Scotland. The cattle boys arrived at her house one day and, in a show of respect for the new Madam, presented her with a large, bloody tongue from a freshly slaughtered cow. It was so fresh, in fact, it was still moving! She was expected to cook this delicacy and eat it. I was already queasy when I heard this story, and when Mandy pointed out one of the cold cuts on the lunch buffet table was indeed tongue, I steered very clear.

Around that time every year, Tengwe put on one of its biggest golfing events of the year, called the Tengwe Masters. People came from all over the country to join in the sport and festivities. The catering for this event required help from everyone, whether it was for the big Saturday night dinner, the Sunday lunch, tea both days, or the "gin tent" on the course. That year I was slated to help in the kitchen, but barely managed to cook a batch of chicken before my morning sickness overcame me and I had to go home.

I found that pregnancy did not suit my body all that well – morning sickness, migraines and carpal tunnel syndrome plagued me badly. The intense, thick smell of smoke in those early days of my pregnancy in the winter made me feel so queasy, that I still associate that smell with pregnancy. During the winter months, with no moisture in the air, the smoke more or less hangs around. Whether it is from the natives cooking or keeping warm, or the burning of fire breaks in fields, or just fields burning because of extreme dry conditions, the amount of smoke in the air is heightened and the odor is concentrated.

As I emerged from that phase and summer was upon us, I fell victim to the cruel affliction of carpal tunnel syndrome. It was the middle of the summer in Africa, and I slept with wool gloves on my hands trying to find some relief from the frozen numbness. We found out that I was carrying a boy and decided to name him James, Andy's first name. He was due at the end of January, and by November I was huge. The heat was intense as we waited for the rains to begin. My brightest light during this time arrived by plane from Bulawayo in the form of a Boston Terrier puppy, whom we christened Ellie. Having spent much time around this unique breed, I longed for one of my own, and Ellie was my first baby. At the time of her introduction on the farm, Sam, Bella, and Cindy were still with us, and eventually she claimed her place among the hierarchy, as well as her place in our bed, as Bostons are known to do.

One day that hot November while Dave and Pete went fishing, I spent the afternoon with Serena in their pool, trying to cool off. They had a small, jellybean shaped pool with steps all around the shallow end. We sat on the steps across from each other, water up to our chests, as the sun was going down. All of a sudden, conversation was interrupted by a splash in front of us. We looked toward the sound, confused by the ripples in the water. Out of nowhere, I felt a wet, slippery snake crawl up my shoulder and up my neck and behind my ear. I heard Serena scream, "It's a snake!" and on instinct, I flung it off me with the back of my hand. I don't know how I pole-vaulted my enormous body out of the water, but the next thing I knew I was lying next to the pool on my side and Serena was repeatedly whacking the snake with a broom she had grabbed from the veranda.

My heart was about to pound out of my chest and I was sure I would go into labor right then and there, when Dave and Pete arrived. I could have killed Dave when his reaction was "Why did you kill it? It's not poisonous!" As it turned out, it was not a venomous snake, but an aggressive natured snake all the same, called a Herald snake, and that particular one was about four feet long and I was glad it was dead.

Snakes were a part of life on the farm, as I was to find out. A quick reaction to the warning "snake bark" of a dog could save its life, and if the bark went unrecognized, it could be too late. Bella was bitten badly by a puff-adder once, and we sped thirty miles to the vet in Karoi for an injection. She recovered after a miserable, swollen week. We lost Freckles and Cindy eventually to cobras, and Dave once shot an Egyptian cobra, one of the deadliest, off our veranda. I myself shot a hovering Boomslung snake Never had spotted in the tree outside the scullery once. Shirley and Andy lost a goose to a fourteen foot python that could not be killed as pythons are considered royal game in Zimbabwe. The natives have a superstition that if you kill a python, the rains will not come. Aubrey learned this only after he had been out with the dogs on one of his visits, and had come across a snake, shot it, and bragged about it. Dave then told him he would be personally responsible if Tengwe got no rain that season!

Chapter 4

As my pregnancy neared its end, I was increasingly eager to get beyond it. The carpal tunnel had reached a level of extreme discomfort. I was fortunate to have a sympathetic friend and neighbor Laurie Dawson, who was practiced in aromatherapy. She volunteered to give me herbal massages on my arms and hands every few days, allowing for a bit of temporary relief. Even Debbie's teenage daughter Jessica, could see how miserable I was and made me what the boarding-school kids called an "End of Term Worm," a calendar of sorts in which each segment of the worm's body represented a day. She had colored it cheerfully and brightly, but I relished tearing every paper section off that worm each day, counting down the days to my due date!

As I was Christmas shopping that year, I took advantage of the newly introduced cell phones that had arrived in Zimbabwe just months earlier. I bought Dave one for Christmas, and it was such a novelty! At first we could only use it while we were in Harare or Chinhoyi, as those were the only places that had towers. Eventually, most of the towns throughout the country were hooked up, and life became a little more convenient, but we never were able to get signal on the farm.

Right before Christmas that year, the Garden Club committee asked if

I would do a presentation on how to prepare and cook an American Goose for Christmas dinner, and any other American traditions I could pass along. I accepted, as it gave me something to focus on in place of my pitiful physical condition.

The pictures from that day are quite funny to look back on. As I gave a speech on how to prepare a goose with a tropical glaze and a fruity stuffing, egg nog (which they had not had before), and brownies for Santa, I actually looked like I had swallowed the whole goose itself. The day ended up to be a huge success, though not for the five geese my mother-in-law had contributed for kitchen testing!

I waddled through the holidays that year, unable to concentrate on anything but my upcoming birth and the logistics of how we would work it out. As Harare was a good two and a half hour drive, the doctors all recommended that we stay in town a week or so prior to the due date. At that time, we did not have a flat of our own in Harare. We chose to stay on the farm and take our chances.

Shortly after Mom arrived in mid-January for the birth of her first grandchild, violent strikes and riots broke out in Harare. This was a reaction to price hikes President Robert Mugabe had implemented on basic commodities, all government controlled products, such as bread, meal, cooking oil and fuel. We were advised to avoid town at all costs, and I missed my weekly appointment two weeks before my due date. Obviously, we were then faced with the question, "What if I go into labor anyway?"

Tensions had been steadily on the rise as a direct result of Mugabe's latest political movements, primarily his Land Resettlement Program which he announced at the end of 1997. According to Mugabe, there were to be five million hectares of commercial farmland designated for resettlement. When the program was first announced, the targets were to be farms of foreign land-owners, underutilized and derelict farms, landowners owning more than one farm, and absentee landowners. This news initially jolted our community, as well as the entire country. No one was quite sure how to take the announcement. "Were they for real?" was the question everyone asked. For us personally, we were forced to shelve our house plans permanently, as it made no sense to invest heavily in a piece of ground that could very likely be taken from us. Deeply disappointed, and emotionally vulnerable in my pregnant state, I wondered for the first time about the security of our future. As a result, Dave and I switched gears and just decided to update the humble house we had. We also then vowed to start sending as much money as we could possibly afford out of the country every year.

After the reaction to the price increases, Mugabe uncharacteristically backed down, probably more from the international pressure he was receiving, as the IMF and World Bank had just proclaimed that he would be forced to pay the farmers' compensation for the land he planned to take, and could only do so in a "willing buyer, willing seller" situation. It was a huge relief to us to hear that Harare was calm, because three days before my due date, I conveniently began having contractions in the car about forty-five minutes outside Harare, as we were on our way to my weekly appointment. I was sent to the hospital immediately upon my arrival at the doctor's office.

Compared to the painful pregnancy I had endured, labor was relatively easy for me. The only snag came when it was time to insert my epidural. Thinking I was in for hours and hours of labor, I had reached the point when it was time for relief. Mr. Robertson (specialists in Zimbabwe are referred to as "Mr."; common practitioners are called "Dr.") arrived to do the procedure, and I was instructed to lean over my enormous, seriously contracting stomach and to hold very still, which I did, and did, and did, until he got so frustrated with what he called the "blunt third-world needles" that he could not get into my spinal cord properly. By the time he got one in, he had probably poked me ten times and I wished I had just chosen a natural birth. I actually got what I wished for, as the drip for the epidural was also not working properly, another result of cheap and inferior equipment, and James was ready to join the party. Fortunately, it was a quick labor and James was born within three hours. I spent two nights in the Avenues Clinic, where I received good care from competent "sisters," but was unnerved by the lack of sterility and the cockroaches climbing the walls at night. I could not wait to get my baby home to the comfort and cleanliness of my farm.

Because most of my friends were older, I benefited from their wisdom regarding motherhood. Having had a breast reduction at the age of nineteen to reduce extremely cumbersome breasts, I knew my chances of breast-feeding were small. I was hopeful though, when I was able to give James some milk at first, but soon realized it was not nearly enough to satisfy my hungry baby. In tears, I began washing bottles and mixing formula when Serena just happened to walk in my kitchen, as I have mentioned could be a common occurrence. She said, "Why the tears?" Mom explained that we were switching to bottles and she replied, "What a lucky girl you are!" and detailed her own ordeal of cracked and bleeding nipples. She helped me understand that the whole family could then participate in feeding James, and from that day I have never looked back.

As we began to settle in with James, it became apparent that he had colic. My attempts at calming him were futile, yet for several weeks I refused to put him on Irene's back, even after all my friends encouraged it. I now know I could have saved myself weeks of frustration, for I finally gave in and called for Irene. She grabbed a towel and adeptly swung my crying baby on her back, wrapped him tightly with his tummy against her back, his legs and arms hugging her waist inside the securely tied towel, and walked off with a huge smile on her face, patting his bum, as James fell into a deep sleep. And so for the first six months of his life, he napped on Irene's back, wrapped in an "mberecko," for hours while she did her chores. It brought such harmony to the house that I was able to forgive the pungent body odor of my baby as he emerged from the towel, having hugged Irene's warm, sweaty back for hours. On Irene's day off, I would wrap him on my own back for his naps. This practice is second-nature to the natives, who do not have the luxury of bassinets and such, and it was rare to see any woman without a baby on her back. When a second baby would come along, the older one got passed on to an older sibling's back. Serena was actually instructed by her doctor to have her first-born, Lindsay, on the nanny's back as many hours as she could as a remedy to correct the child's underdeveloped hips.

Irene's own daughter lived in the reserve, or Tribal Trust Lands (TTLs), with her grandparents while Irene lived on the farm and worked. It is common practice in the Shona culture that the grandparents actually raise the children, a result of the "Lebola system" that is firmly in place. A lebola, similar to a dowry, is promised and partially paid to the parents of a woman at the time a man asks for her hand in marriage. A plan is then agreed upon whereby the lebola is to be paid in installments. Any children born to that couple belong to the parents of the bride until the lebola is fully paid off. Ideally, the lebola should be paid at the time of childbirth, as technically the woman has then proven her worth, as such. In Irene's case, her baby was born out of wedlock, so no lebola was in place, and the parents kept the child in hopes of selling her when she came of age. Because the grandparents own the children, they often request they live with them. The schooling was generally cheaper in the reserves and the children could help with crops in the fields. These TTLs were large tracts of land the government owned and entrusted to the local chiefs. Many rural natives are settled there and given plots to grow crops, though they do not own title to the land and were therefore beholden to the whims of the chief and the government.

Kimi, age eight, was so pleased with her little brother, and I was grateful she was around as she taught me how to fold the cloth nappies we used, and fed James bottles. She was a great helper. She had a little sister at home, so she was actually more experienced than I. (More than anything, I believe she was just thrilled that Dave and I had a boy, so as to not disturb her secure position as Daddy's little girl.) Amongst all this activity, Dave had decided that we not only needed a new baby, but it that was also time for a new pointer. Geena, a long-eared puppy, joined our family a week before James arrived, bringing the total number of dogs back to five at that time.

When James was about a month old, we took him for his first outing (and mine), as it was Pete Mason's fortieth birthday and Debbie and Leith Bray were having a dinner by the dam to celebrate. This was such a treat that I refused to miss out, even if it meant I would be tending to a crying baby all night. A long dining table was set up on the edge of their beautiful dam, a picturesque setting we enjoyed many times over the years. Debbie had cooked an elegant dinner for about twenty five people, and we had a grand time, mainly because James slept in the car for the first time in his life for three whole hours.

Chapter 5

The house took on a new routine after James' arrival, and we were all adjusting. As Irene was spending so much time helping me with James, I took on another nanny to help Louie with the housework, named Memory. She had come looking for a job as she was a qualified Health Worker, but as the farm already employed one, I hired her for the house. As the garden had grown, Never also needed help. We hired his cousin Jesphat to assist him outside. We had expanded the vegetable garden and were successful in growing all the gourmet lettuces, as well as tons of herbs and vegetables. I was very attached to and reliant on my staff and considered them part of the family. I shopped weekly in order to keep my house staff supplied with tea, sugar, milk and bread. I gave each of them bars of soap to encourage personal hygiene, something they tended to neglect. After James was born, the entire house staff got raises, as I knew all the work would increase. Louie and Irene became invaluable to me, and I felt very close to all of them. My Shona was improving slowly, although we had all reached a point where we could understand each other. They came to know my ways, and I believe they were very happy in their jobs.

The farm workforce was such a crucial part of our lives in so many ways. As I have said, most of the families had been on Dendera Farm for generations and was its own little community. There were managers, foremen and casual workers, each having his or her own place in a type of understood hierarchy that they all accepted. The house staff enjoyed a higher status than a field worker, and the farm manager, Timot, presided over everyone except for Dave and Andy. Dave was younger than most of his permanent employees, but it was obvious how he had gained their respect over the years as he was an extremely fair and compassionate boss. More importantly, Dave has a complete and total grasp of the Shona language, which he learned from birth as he spent most of his childhood running around the farm with all the little black boys as playmates. The workers trusted Dave, often referring to him as "Baba," or father. So often, he was the one they turned to for help and guidance. More than once, Dave would have to rush off to Karoi in the middle of the night with a woman experiencing a difficult childbirth, or sort out a variety of domestic disputes, or administer medicine to a sick child. Part of the Shona culture is extremely superstitious, and sometimes rivaling families would resort to a type of "black magic." A random medicine bottle with an unknown substance and an odd top could be rigged up and left around the house grounds, signifying that a terrible spell had been placed on that family. They believed in it wholeheartedly, and Dave would have to sit down with all parties involved and work through it. There were self-proclaimed witch-doctors, "nganga" in Shona, around the district, and people sought them out at times, but Dave and Andy strongly discouraged any of them coming onto our farm, much less living there.

With so many little nuances, it was common for jealousies to occur, as I found out. Once, I was baking some cookies and had so many on hand, that

I gave a bundle to Never as he was leaving for the day. Someone found out, got very jealous, and reported a false story to the police that he had attacked his wife. It was a headache for Never, and he was released, but it could happen so easily over small things. When Dave explained their ways to me, I adjusted my own, and if ever I wanted to give leftover food to my staff, I gave it to Louie to divide up as he saw fit, being the highest rank in the house.

After James' birth, Shirley and Andy bought a flat in Harare, so that we could have somewhere to stay when we went to town. It was a huge convenience, as Irene could go with us, and we were able to leave her with James while we did our errands. Trips to town were usually very rushed, as a list would accumulate over two weeks, and then it all had to be done in two days. This could include anything from haircuts and doctors appointments to grocery shopping and farm shopping. We shopped in bulk for most things, but by that time, Debbie and Gill had taken over the Tengwe Butchery and truly made all our lives so much easier by providing a place where we could buy quality meat, dairy products and liquor right in Tengwe.

Throughout that next year, I became more and more involved in the community and around the farm. Apart from doing all the wages and the accounts, I was in charge of the farm "Health Worker." Each month she would come to me to collect a supply of preventative malaria medicine, salt tablets, pain reliever and condoms. She kept a written record of who was taking what kinds of medicines and was available for the employees when they were at work. AIDS is such a problem among the African natives, with lack of education and understanding about the disease being the primary cause for the high number of cases. Zimbabwe is particularly susceptible and actually leads the continent with the highest number of AIDS cases in Africa. I kept the Health Worker stocked with condoms and literature, and hoped it would help at least someone, but I can't say that it really made a big difference – their beliefs and practices were pretty set. Ironically, Memory, the so-called Health Worker, became a victim of AIDS.

One year at Christmas, I held a house competition on the farm with big prize money. Everyone participated, and I spent an entire day walking around the four compounds inspecting houses. Each family had a three-room brick house, with a separate mud hut for the kitchen, and most were very house-proud. The grounds were dirt but always swept with homemade brooms and kept tidy. Many had some plants or flowers growing nearby, and they used different color clays and charcoal to draw patterns on the huts. I was impressed and amazed at the way they lived. Water was brought in large buckets on the women's heads from the dams that were close to each compound. A fire had to be lit for cooking, and laundry was all done by hand. The only source of light was candles and torches, and there was no refrigeration. One of their delicacies is sour milk – they love it! My staff was always delighted when our milk would go rotten after several days in the fridge.

The life of an African woman is a tough one indeed, for not only does she work, but she is in charge of all the housework, child-rearing and cooking. Often, I would see heavily pregnant women, sometimes with a baby strapped on the back, working in the fields. I felt weak and spoiled to think how I had pampered my pregnant body, and even more so when Dave related stories of women actually giving birth right there in the field, and returning to work the next day with the baby on her back, of course! When I questioned this practice, Dave told me that they actually chose to work in that condition, not wanting to miss a day's wage. Only the men in the family were hired as permanent employees; the women were offered jobs as temporary, or casual, employees when work was available.

Irene found herself in that precarious situation of being pregnant out of wedlock once again when James was about three years old. I knew she had been dating one of the policemen from the township, and after some time, I noticed the suggestive swell under her maids' uniform. On her slight figure, there was no hope of disguising a pregnant belly. When I finally confronted her, she denied vehemently that she was pregnant. I was just about to leave for the States, and when I came back six weeks later, she had no choice but to admit the truth. She came to me in woeful tears, saying she had seen the "nganga" to terminate her pregnancy, but his "muti" had failed. I felt so sorry for her and convinced her that all would be well. She ended up having a baby girl, named Gracious, who came to work with Irene on her back everyday. While she was on maternity leave, Memory became James' nanny, but I had already noticed several dark purple and blue lesions on her recently and became wary of how much time James spent with her. She adored him so much, and many times I had to stop her from kissing him. Some years later, Memory actually did die of AIDS.

Dave was all set to install electricity in each compound, a great expense and improvement, but the project was continually postponed as the political instability increased. One important indicator we had that things were declining was the foreign exchange rate. As I mentioned, Dave and I bought as much foreign exchange as we could afford and wired it all to the United States. That August was Dave's fortieth birthday, which we celebrated in conjunction with James' christening, as Mom and Aubrey were out for a visit. James was six months old and very much a precious and doted on baby. For Dave's birthday, I had been working secretly to buy a new motor for his bass boat, his pride and joy. I received a quote from a dealer in Karoi and was told it would cost $1500 U. S dollars. The rate when he quoted me was eighteen to one, making my bill $27,000 Zim dollars. This was expensive for us, but a sacrifice I was prepared to make as I knew the delight a new motor would bring. By the time the motor cleared customs ten days later, the rate had slipped to twenty-seven to one, and I had to pay $43,000 Zim dollars.

Chapter 6

That year, we were unable to join the group going back to
Mozambique, as James was too small to take on such a journey. Instead,
Dave and I planned a two-week holiday at the Kariba house for the end of
September. The sales were over by then, and there was a lull on the farm
before planting was to begin. We packed the car with all the baby
equipment, supplies and Irene. I had learned that if Never dug up nine or ten
lettuce plants and potted them in plastic sleeves, we could have fresh lettuce
everyday at Kariba, as long as I kept the plants on the upstairs veranda so the
elephants couldn't reach them. The baboons did get to them sometimes,
though.

That particular holiday, although it was a bit of a consolation prize,
turned out to be one of our best. That time of year is the hottest at Kariba,
but it is also the best time for tiger fishing. Our routine for the two weeks
was to wake very early and go fishing, returning for breakfast and a swim
with James, who was then eight months old. We went on game drives to see
the impala, waterbuck, buffalo and whoever else was roaming around the

plains. Late afternoon fishing trips and booze cruises were the habit for the end of the day. There is a welcome condition one catches at the lake called "Kariba fever" and we certainly got it that trip – the heat, sun and water all work together to instill that relaxed laziness of a true holiday. Because the rains had not begun, the game was quite concentrated around the lush bush near the lake, and we were visited everyday by the elephants drinking from the splash pool at the house and the usual wave of buck and hippo in the evening. Late one night, Dave was awakened by the warning bark of a bush buck on the lawn outside our window. (We were sleeping downstairs with James this trip.) His keen bush training told him something was amiss, and he quietly woke me to come see. A domestic cat was sitting in the windowsill of the open living-room window, and as we followed the gaze of the bush buck, a leopard soundlessly appeared on the steps of the veranda, not ten yards from us, stalking the housecat. The cat saved itself by jumping through the burglar bars into the house, and the leopard calmly walked off, leaving us astounded by the rare scene we had witnessed.

That incident, though extraordinary in itself, was one of many examples I can cite to prove how Dave taught me so much about the nature and animals of Africa. He taught me that I had to see and hear differently than I had before, and though it took me a long time to understand, I did come to appreciate the intricate ways of the natural world in which we lived. He taught me to listen to the birds so that I actually heard them. My favorite sound was the morning call of the Coucal bird, a very plain looking, average sized, brown bird. Every morning in the summer, I would lie in bed and listen to the calming call that sounded like the echo of water flowing through a cave. The repetitive call of the doves and the ever-present, persistent "go-away" bird became permanent background music in my head. I learned the habits of the cattle and came to know the process of how they were grown and marketed. I lamented with the "weaners" when they bellowed incessantly for days (and nights) after being separated from their mothers. Dave dearly loved working with the cattle, even when he had to pull a breached calf from a cow's uterus, which happened fairly regularly. I learned that the magnificent kudu could become addicted to nicotine. On daily morning tours around the tobacco lands, we found many of the tender young plants had been cropped. I learned that the cheekiest animal of all is a mother hippo protecting her babies. Once we watched a hippo charge an enormous elephant bull who had come too close to her pod in the water.

I also came to appreciate the landscape of Zimbabwe as a character in itself, affecting lives on many levels. There was always a constant challenge to keep up with nature on the farm. During long stretches with no rain, Dave would have the workers build small dams in between the rows of tobacco, in order to block any precious drops of water from running off. In contrast, the rain would come in droves and the job would be to break those same dams to avoid water-logging. Many farmers in Tengwe had enough water on their farms to irrigate, but we were dry farmers and relied solely on the weather to nourish our crops. There were many times when my friends would literally be house-bound by over-running rivers because of too much rain. On more than one occasion, Dave had to totally abandon sections of crops simply because the tractors could not get in and out. They had been through many drought years, but during my time there was only plentiful rain, sometimes too much. We religiously recorded every drop of rain that fell on our farm, as did all farmers. Interestingly, most Zimbabwean farmers would agree that it is far less challenging to farm in drier years than excessively wet ones.

The effect the rain had on our lives was absolute and indisputable. Dave awoke every morning of his life checking the sky and the direction of the wind. The window above our bathroom sink was as accurate as any forecast around – a north wind blew directly in our faces through that window, indicating oncoming rain. The local weather forecast was vague and unreliable, and CNN didn't really concentrate on our neck of the woods. Major thunderstorms more often than not caused power outages, and depending on what was damaged, these outages could go on for days. Generators were crucial, as the fires in the curing barns had to be kept going or we would lose the entire barn of tobacco, and we generally had freezers stocked full of meat. Another negative effect of excessive rain was the fact that our struggling party-line telephone system would inevitably go out at the first threat of rain, or even just distant thunder and lightening. It was extremely frustrating during these times, but there was nothing to be done except report the outage and wait for the phone company to get around to fixing your line. It could take weeks sometimes. We eventually were upgraded to a digital phone system and managed to get dial-up email and internet access, which made a huge difference. Within Tengwe, we had a radio system which allowed us to speak to anyone within a thirty-five mile radius. I could spend an entire morning radioing friends just to see who had a phone that was working so that I could go to their house to make a necessary phone call.

We never really liked to complain about the rain too much as it was so vital to our livelihood. We just coped with the consequences and enjoyed the healthy crops it provided.

Chapter 7

Shortly after that Kariba trip, I was preparing for my first overseas trip back to the US with James, who was nine months old. James, Gill Moolman, and I boarded a plane in Harare bound for London and then on to North Carolina. I had persuaded Gill to come with me as she had never left the continent of Africa before in her life. We were to spend the month of November visiting Mom in High Point, my friends in New York, Aubrey in Washington, and some time at the North Carolina coast. James got off to a rocky start on the plane, screaming his head off, but thanks to a magical "muti" (medicine) for sale in Zimbabwe called Stopayne, he was able to sleep a lot of the way and became a seasoned traveler by the end of the trip.

I had great fun in seeing Gill's reaction to certain aspects of life in the US. She was surprised to see white men working road construction and collecting trash. She was amazed that someone could be trusted to "pay at the pump." The choices in the grocery store were overwhelming to her, and I must admit, on my trips back to the U.S., I also found the choices on the shelves to be overkill at times.

I continued to travel back to the States with James periodically, usually with Dave, as I was determined that Mom and her grandson would have a strong bond. She came to the farm every July and August, and we worked a system where it would generally be no longer than six months in between visits. My trips back increasingly highlighted my personal distance from the American culture. More and more, trips "home" would center more around time with my family than with long lost friends. So many times I found myself unable to find common ground with some friends, and many of those undernourished relationships eventually faded away. I believe this had a lot to do with the fact that I had chosen to leave our social circle at a crucial and pivotal time in life. I got married, had a baby, and settled in my first home in a country and community so far removed from what we had known, that to try to relate and compare these experiences was futile. I had found happiness in what would be deemed a backward and undeveloped society, but I came to know that the meaning of those terms is all relative. The thought often occurred to me that I was so lucky to have the best of both worlds. Fortunately, I have a small, core group of friends who remain close to me today.

My favorite thing to do on my trips to America was to buy items for my friends and staff that were not available in Zimbabwe. I was constantly stocking up on Ziploc baggies, Nestle Chocolate Chips, prepared horseradish, and flavored coffees for myself. I used to take brightly colored flip-flops and built-in bra tops home for my girlfriends, the latest in fishing tackle for the men, and even shin guards for my garden boys. Dendera Farm sported a soccer team that competed every Sunday afternoon. As Never was one of the star players, we switched his work schedule around so that he could play every game. Because he consistently came to work on Mondays with bruised and bleeding shins from the games, he was thrilled to have shin guards. Louie usually got a new watch (He once asked for a Rolex! Needless to say, he got a fake.) or new shoes, and Irene and Memory would get clothes, nighties and underwear. I loved seeing their delight in their presents. I never came home to a house that had not been scrubbed from head to toe, carpets washed, windows cleaned and fresh flowers in the house. My staff was as house-proud as I was and took great pleasure in seeing my satisfaction.

Chapter 8

One major aspect of our lives that was growing along with James was Dave's increasing passion for bass fishing. The dams in Zimbabwe are famous in Southern Africa for their abundance of big largemouth bass. He and his friends were all avid fishermen, but Dave is a naturally skilled fisherman unlike many. He dominated the small league he fished in Karoi, and performed consistently in the national tournaments that were held five times a year. Extensive practice and preparation were necessary to compete on that level, and he spent many long weekends away from home. His fishing partner, Johno Coast, was as passionate as Dave, and together they camped all over the country in their quest for bass. I became a textbook fishing widow, along with some other friends, but we usually made the most of our girl-time while the men were away. The most inconvenient part of Dave's fishing trips was that he and Johno insisted on taking Never on every trip, as he was so good at setting up camp, cleaning the boat and cooking breakfast and dinner. I hated not having him around. Although Louie and Irene were capable of running the house, things in the garden did not get done, and the fire in the boiler was not kept running the way I liked when

Never was away. I used to scream my head off when I did not have hot water for a shower.

I seldom chose to camp with Dave on those trips, but the wives did manage a few fun weekends when the venue had comfortable accommodation. A large dam outside Harare, called Mazvikadei, is a scenic retreat with many large homes. We rented a house during one of the tournaments that housed five families, complete with a swimming pool. Another trip Mandy and I made was to the lowveld in the southern region of the country, a good eight hour drive from Tengwe. Situated among the sugar fields was a beautiful dam called Mtiri. Dave and Jamie fished while Mandy, James and I relaxed at the lodge or on the boat. This particular trip showed that James (age three) could catch fish with the big boys. Jamie still will not admit to this day that James caught better and bigger fish than he did, but I have the photos to prove it.

Dave's dedication and time paid off as he competed for and won a spot on the Zimbabwean team, which traveled to the United States every year to participate in an international competition. In 1999, Dave placed first on the team in the Divisionals which took place on the Tom Bigbee Waterway in Columbus, Mississippi, and in doing so, qualified to fish in the B.A.S.S. National Championship the following year. I was extremely proud of all his accomplishments, but his time away from home during James' first year was quite challenging for me. Fortunately, I had great support from my friends and family, and was never alone unless I wanted to be while Dave was away. During some of those weekends, James and I would sleep at Shirley and Andy's, but often I would stay by myself. Because there had been a marked increase in theft and break-ins in the area, security was a growing concern. The rising inflation was taking a toll on the poorer people who were desperate to feed themselves and their families. A friend of ours had opened a new security firm in Tengwe and had asked Dave if he could base his guards on our farm, as we were the most centrally located farm in Tengwe. At the end of the road leading to our driveway, Dave built a facility that housed a crew of five or six guards who were on call by radio for any Tengwe situation. Their presence brought me much security during those nights alone, but I never slept without a loaded shotgun beside me. This was a routine I had learned from Dave, who was unable to sleep, ever, without his trusted twelve-gauge gun by his head, a carry-over habit from his war days.

After the excitement of winning the spot to represent Zimbabwe in the championship waned, we realized what a financial burden it would be for us. I immediately planned a fundraiser for October of that year and brought Halloween to Tengwe, a holiday unheard of in Zim. Weeks of preparation went into this event, and I engaged the help of my good friends once again. Mandy, with her incredible artistic talents, was in charge of the decorations. The main hall of the club transformed into a haunted Halloween scene to rival any. Hundreds of bats and ghosts dangled from the ceiling, a haunted house structure was erected to serve as the bar, gravestones and papier mache jack-o-lanterns decorated the walls and floors. Sue and Serena, experienced caterers, were my right arm in the kitchen. Sharon, Gill and Debbie were the organizers of the children's meal, a raffle, "bobbing for apples" and the piñata. I organized a series of themed tents to be set up all over the club grounds, and each B.A.S.S. league member had to dress up as scary monsters or witches and receive the trick-or-treaters at their tents. Meyer was frighteningly memorable as a witch, and succeeded in scaring the daylights out of the little children. As with all our functions, an event of this nature could never be pulled off without help from the many willing bodies. I do not think those kids had ever seen so much candy in their lives; I really went overboard a bit. There were even empty tents with a convenient supply of shaving cream and toilet paper for tricking! After all the games, the adults enjoyed a catered three course meal and my friend Heather the DJ provided the tunes for all-night dancing. We ended up having a blast and raising enough money to cover almost all of Dave's expenses on his trip. This was my first taste of true large-scale catering and entertaining, and I really got the bug. It was that next year that Mandy and I took over the Entertainment committee at the club.

Following the Halloween party, Dave threw himself into his work with the planting season upon us, and we all prepared for the holidays and the huge Millennium party that year. Looking back now I see this as a time in our lives of true contentment. We were a successful farming enterprise making a good steady income, we had plans for building our nest-egg for the future, we had a balanced life we filled with the activities we enjoyed, we were blessed with beautiful, healthy children and a precious circle of friends, and a supportive family. Pictures from the New Year's Eve black-tie affair under a massive tent on the club cricket pitch that year show relaxed smiles on bright faces, a community looking forward to what the new Millennium would bring. These farmers were excellent at pinpointing the signs of upcoming weather systems, but not one predicted this particular "calm before the storm."

Chapter 9

I celebrated my 29th birthday on February 1st, 1999, and on that day I received one of the grandest presents I have ever gotten. Although I had made significant progress with my gardening skills, I always maintained that I would never be able to successfully grow a rose; such a complex and intimidating flower was beyond my immature capabilities and I was sure to kill it. Serena arrived that day with five home-grown rose bushes, pre-mixed chemical sprays, fertilizers, and a folder containing pages of typed instructions on how to grow and nurture a rose.

Of course, I had no choice but to plant them, according to the specific instructions, and did so the very next day. Never dug five holes one meter by one meter wide, by one meter deep and we followed directions until all the bushes were in place and fed properly. From the day my first bud appeared and then opened to reveal its beauty and grandeur, I was hooked. I consulted anyone who would give advice on rose-growing tips and committed the entire center of my round-about driveway to roses. I followed a strict regimen of spraying and feeding, pruning and dead-heading. These bushes became my pride and joy, and I am forever grateful to my dear friend for introducing me to what has become a fulfilling passion in my life.

We also celebrated James' first birthday that January, invested in a four-wheeler, and broke ground for the new guest cottage that was to be built in the yard. The four wheeler was an upgrade on Dave's motorbike, a cumbersome bike I had not been able to master. The steady four wheeler, on the other hand, became my favorite toy. I found that riding around the farm always cured any fussy spells James had; we covered many a mile aimlessly joy-riding through the fields or visiting Granny and Papa. I even became immune to the spray of mombie (cow) poop that splattered on my legs as we went through the cattle fields! One of our favorite activities was to ride out to the mealie (corn) fields and pick fresh green mealies for lunch. I learned that a corn cob was an excellent teething tool – it satisfied on many levels. When James did grow teeth, he could not get enough of the succulent cobs freshly picked from the field. Once, James and I were picking a basketful of mealies, and the crop guard actually reported us to Dave!

We had designed a two-bedroom, 1 1/2 bath cottage, mainly to accommodate Mom, who spent most of July and August with us every year. The farm builder, Livingstone, and Dave produced a charming little carriage house that was just perfect for our needs. It was handy that Dave was so knowledgeable in the plumbing field and was able to produce functioning loos, showers, sinks and septic tanks on his own. We also extended the roof to cover a portion of the veranda of the main house and resurfaced its cement flooring using a method of scoring dyed cement to take on the enhanced look of terra-cotta tiles. Tim and Laurie Dawson had a farm builder who was skilled in this practice, and they were kind enough to let us borrow him for a few days to complete the job. Kimi moved into the old guest room, and James upgraded to a room of his own, not a nursery. The door outside his room that led to our office became his growth ruler, and we took great delight in marking his height every three to four months with a measurement in centimeters and the date. This was all part of the expansion plan as there were still many rumblings about the future of the farms in Zimbabwe.

We also improved upon the burglar bars that were on the windows and added metal doors to the bedroom section of the house. The entire bedroom and office area was totally secure when those doors and windows were locked. I had become immune to the unsightly bars as far as appearance went; the security they provided was far more important.

During Mom's visit that July, I gave her a trip to Victoria Falls for her sixtieth birthday, as neither of us had been there yet. Shirley kept James, as Dave was away fishing, and we flew from the Kariba airport down the length of the lake, and into Vic Falls, where we had two fascinating days. Upon our arrival at the newest hotel to open in the Falls, the Kingdom, we discovered that the opening ceremonies were to take place the next day. Robert Mugabe, along with his Mercedes motorcade, helicopters, and large force of security guards, was in town for the proceedings. I was shocked to open the curtains of our room to find a uniformed guard, armed with a large AK-47, staring back at me through the window to our room! As we walked around the hotel grounds, I saw guards in front of every guest room, an example of Mugabe's growing paranoia. Victoria Falls itself was all that it promised to be, truly a breathtaking sight. The native translation for Victoria Falls is "Mosi au tunya," the smoke that thunders, and that is an accurate description indeed. It is heard and felt before being seen, and once beheld, it is mesmerizing in its presence and power.

We had dinner at the Victoria Falls Hotel, a famously grand hotel and one of the last bastions of British colonialism in the country. Vaulted ceilings, plush red velvet curtains, life-size portraits of British officers, mounted game trophies, historical artifacts from the days of Cecil Rhodes and Ian Smith define the atmosphere of this grandiose venue with its sprawling, meticulously manicured gardens. In contrast, the Kingdom Hotel was an ethnically decorated tribute to the native culture of Zimbabwe, full of wooden carvings, brightly colored cloths and soapstone statues. The town of Victoria Falls itself was not what I had expected, as I had envisioned more commercialization, but really the main attractions there are the actual Falls, the beauty of the Zambezi River and the game it houses. We spotted a rare black rhinoceros on a booze cruise, an animal I had not seen before then. The tourists all seemed to be enjoying themselves, but we didn't really consider ourselves tourists and I suppose were immune to many of the aspects of Africa they found interesting and unusual.

Dave and Ann Beattie's wedding day

Dave and James at Lake Mtiri

James and Irene

Dave and Ann on the original safari

Floating on the Zambezi River - Birthday weekend at Kockott's Camp

Farm workers in the Grading Shed

James, Kimi and Dave at Lake Kariba

Shamisu and James going hunting

Louie in the kitchen

Never cleaning kudu horns

December 2006 trip home

Kimi and James, Debbie Bray and Ann, Jamie and Mandy Saul, Sharon and Andy Kockott

PART FOUR

CHINJA

Chapter 1

In the months leading up to the Millennium in 1999 and in the first part of 2000, Zimbabwe experienced what seems now like a series of tremors, a foreboding of troubled times ahead. Since the end of the civil war in 1980, the land issue had been an ever-present concern for all of Zimbabwe and its citizens. Instead of redistributing the land, as he had promised the people in his war campaign, Mugabe and his cronies exploited the economy they had inherited, ruled as elite chiefs and profited from the successful farming enterprises the white farmers provided. Directly after independence, there was a limited amount of resettlement among the landless, but not nearly enough to satisfy the hundreds of thousands who lived in poverty in the rural areas. These original resettlement farms were largely unsuccessful because of lack of technical and agricultural skill and financial support that was supposedly to come from the government.

In 1992, the government passed the Land Acquisition Act (a timely move running up to an election) in an attempt to redistribute the land again, this time with no compensation. The Commercial Farmers' Union (CFU) as well as the IMF strongly opposed the process of illegal redistribution. At that time, there was already a measure in place that any person selling a farm had to first get a "letter of no interest" from the government stating that they had no intentions to acquire the piece of land in question. Many farms were indeed purchased by the government on a "willing buyer, willing seller" basis, and although not all of those properties purchased by the government actually went to the landless peasants as they should have, it was a legal way of acquiring land and compensating the farmer for the improvements to the property. Mugabe tended to use the land issue as a trump card in order to gain support among the rural population, the largest in the country, but he failed to make good on his promises. This time was no different as the government let the issue fizzle out once again, though throughout the 1990's, opposition grew steadily as millions faced poverty and starvation. The Land Resettlement Programs of 1997 and 1998 followed along the same lines as the previous attempts to gain political support on the ground through his powerful rhetoric, and yet no action was taken.

Many factors contributed to the eventual demise of the Zimbabwean economy, none more so than simple government corruption and mismanagement. Robert Mugabe made a series of political decisions that had dire consequences for his country including his failure to comply with IMF demands and measures for economic reform as part of an agreement on yet another squandered loan. By 1995, unemployment had tripled and inflation was at fifty percent. He had entered into an incredibly expensive and costly war in the Congo in order to secure his share of the rich resources the diamond and cobalt mines produced. This war was extremely unpopular at home as so many domestic issues were ignored and quality of life declined. His answer to protests and strikes was to just declare them illegal; he placed bans on the media in order to muzzle the news of his actions. He allowed the CIO (Central Intelligence Organization) to arrest and torture innocent civilians for voicing dissenting opinions. The economy was in trouble and foreign investors became increasingly wary as government tenders and contracts were consistently granted to high-ranking officials within his ZANU-PF party, and the value of the Zimbabwe dollar spiraled to ridiculous proportions. Since independence in 1980, Mugabe had been paying many of the War Veterans who had backed him in that war a monthly pension. In 1999, because of the climbing inflation and the devaluation of the dollar, these same war veterans demanded more money from the government. Mugabe gave in to their demands and paid an exorbitant sum of over three billion Zimbabwe dollars to appease them, an act that crippled an already faltering economy even more. To further outrage, in spite of the plight of the majority of the people in his country, Mugabe awarded his cabinet ministers with a three hundred percent pay increase as well that year.

Amidst this backdrop of growing opposition in February 2000, Mugabe, needing to intensify his grip on power, declared that the Constitution needed reform. While all sides agreed that reform was indeed necessary, no one outside the government agreed with Mugabe's specific agenda. His main intention was to make further changes to allow himself another ten years in office as President, to take land without compensation, and to declare all government officials immune to prosecution for any illegal crimes committed while in office. Public forums were held to debate the changes under the guise that the voice of the people would actually be heard, but in the end, Mugabe tried to rush through his own constitution, one that did not address the crucial issue of presidential tenure. This blueprint was unacceptable to almost all, including his own party faithful. At the ZANU-PF congress that year, it was decided to call for a referendum vote to determine whether to accept or reject his new constitution. The shocking result was a resounding seventy percent negative response. This was the wake-up call to Robert Mugabe that he was losing power and influence over his people. Parliamentary elections were just six months away at that time, and the MDC opposition party, under the leadership of Morgan Tsvangirai, was gaining strength and support throughout the country. Mugabe then began planning and scheming a course of action that has destroyed lives, families, land and country.

Chapter 2

So there we were, ticking happily along with life, when news of the referendum outcome came to Tengwe. As a farming community and a small percentage of the population, we really had no part in the politics of ZANU-PF, but we were surprised and pleased to hear that Mugabe had not been able to bulldoze his bit of unjust legislation, as he had done so many times in the past. I think we were as surprised as Mugabe himself. At any rate, we took the news in stride. Serena and I had taken the Tengwe Garden Club chairlady and secretary positions, and we planned the February meeting that year around Valentine's Day, complete with a fashion show of clothes from a store in Karoi, a flower arranging lesson by our talented friend Debbie Black, and a recipe booklet I had put together of Garden Club members' favorites for a romantic dinner.

There was nothing romantic, however, about the appearance of a drunken, frenzied mob of at least one hundred people, bearing axes and spears, outside Gill and Meyer's gate days after the referendum result was announced. News of similar farm invasions from other districts around the country began to filter in throughout the last two weeks of February. Robert Mugabe made it clear to the public, as well as to a stricken farming community, where he stood, declaring the white farmers of Zimbabwe "Enemies of the State" in a public address. He blamed the whites for every problem the country had, and vowed that any opponents to his ZANU-PF party would face death, as would we, the white farmers, if we resisted the compulsory acquisition of our land. The MDC was gaining much momentum and was a serious threat to the ruling party, with a strong slogan being chanted and repeated around the country: "Chinja!" (meaning "Change!"). With their backs against the wall, Mugabe and his henchmen put into play one of the most savage, malicious and brutal campaigns Zimbabwe has ever seen.

The lead up to the general election, from February 2000 to June 2000, was a period of extreme violence targeted at the MDC members, supporters and sympathizers. The intimidation on the farms was unbearable. In Gill and Meyer's case, they were not even the landowners. They managed the farming enterprise for the Dawson family of Tengwe. The mob outside their house kept them awake for weeks on end with chanting, screaming, and mayhem all night long. Just to drive in and out of the driveway was enough to bring about a series of violent threats. The farm workforce was targeted even more, as they were more vulnerable to the angry mobs. The government sponsored groups to come to talk to our farm workers, trying to convince them that we were their enemy, that they would have our homes and farms if they voted ZANU-PF, that the whites were the root of all evil, and then followed up with violent threats if they did not comply. Almost nightly, farm workers were attacked, raped, or humiliated and intimidated at the very least.

These mobs were comprised of self-proclaimed war veterans, but in actuality, only one or two true war vets led each mob. Most of the people involved were far too young to have even fought in the war. It was clearly government orchestrated violence. They were paid and fed by the government as they kept their posts. The police had been instructed not to interfere or react to any calls for help from white farmers or MDC supporters, and no crimes of trespassing, property destruction, assault, rape or murder were prosecuted. All the war vets were operating under the assumption that when the farms they invaded were eventually evacuated, they could make themselves at home in our bedrooms. Many times, farmers would go to work and find a plot on one of their fields marked out by wooden pegs, with a war vet standing nearby to say, "This is my farm now." Small grass huts were erected as well, usually right near the homestead, for maximum intimidation.

As I watched Gill and Meyer suffer through their daily ordeal, I could see the toll it took on them. Several other families in Tengwe experienced the same trauma, and all of Tengwe began to question the future. Not surprisingly, many different opinions arose about how to react to the situation and how best to deal with the war veterans and how to proceed forward. During weekly Farmers' Association meetings, heated discussions took place as the men debated varying tactics. There were those who felt that patience, non-aggression and negotiation were the way to go, and others who felt that a united, forceful, unyielding stance was the only way to proceed. In an effort to compromise, an attempt was made by the ZJRI (Zimbabwe Joint Resettlement Initiative) who actually complied a list of about one million hectares farmers from around the country were willing to give the government, for free, for their resettlement scheme. In the end, it became apparent that this underutilized land was not nearly as attractive to the government thieves who preferred the developed farms with their comfortable homes and other amenities. In the beginning, though, I believe everyone shared the feeling that the redistribution scheme would not be followed through to its utmost, that a portion of land would be lost, but that we would be able to sustain our livelihoods, homes and enterprises. After all, the commercial farmers were the very backbone of the Zimbabwean economy, accounting for more than sixty percent of the GDP/export/foreign exchange, and these were the farms that provided at least seventy-five percent of the food for a population of over twelve million.

When the government began issuing Section 5 notices, seemingly at random, tensions increased dramatically. A system was set in place whereby *The Herald*, the government-run newspaper, published a list of designated properties every Friday. At that time, those properties were considered formally, legally and officially "designated," and it was the sole responsibility of the farmer to find out if his property was on the list. A Section 5 notice simply stated that your property was designated for resettlement by the government and, from that time, was in effect owned by the government. Instead of Fridays being the day when the kids came home from school, they turned into a day where hopes and futures hung in the balance. Pete and Serena picked their children up from school in Karoi one week and grabbed a paper at the same time to find that their farm was one of the hundreds from all over the country listed for resettlement that week. I counted ourselves lucky as we had not been affected on our farm yet, but the fear and panic in the air was for everyone.

I was so unsettled by all this activity and could not stop asking – Are they for real? How can a government just come in and make someone give up all they have? How could this happen? Obviously, my free world thinking did not mesh with third-world politics, certainly not the likes of a tyrannical dictator like Robert Mugabe. I can remember people telling me "Don't worry, we have seen this before. Everything will be OK." Dave was not as reassuring as some of the others, as he was very skeptical about what was happening, but at the same time he was not all "gloom and doom" as some. So really, I did not know what to think about the direction our future would take. I was not experienced enough in African politics to know then that such a chaotic movement the war veterans personified could actually take hold. A ridiculous wooden peg in the middle of a fifteen acre field was, in my eyes, just an innocuous item that could easily be removed. It seemed to me that as farmers and landowners we should indeed stand up to these fools. Why not, when so much was at stake?

What changed my view fairly quickly was something I had taken for granted my entire life – the rule of law and order. Lawlessness became the law of the land; police were nonexistent as far as the farmers and MDC supporters were concerned. The police force had been specifically instructed NOT to respond to the calls of white farmers. With no recourse available, we could only rely on ourselves, our community and our neighbors for support.

For Dave and me, our distraction at that time was our upcoming, preplanned trip to the United States for Dave to fish in the B.A.S.S. National Championship. Kimi was coming with us this time, and we had great things planned for her first visit to America, including Disneyworld. We left amongst so much turmoil at home, and I felt deeply torn that we were abandoning our community in a time of ambivalence and uncertainty for all involved.

Once we landed, the weight and stress of the problems on the farm eased but never left us completely as we received word, via the email, that more and more farms were being invaded and looted, and more and more people were being attacked and murdered. We checked in frequently with Shirley and Andy to get updates, and none of it was positive. The first white farmer, David Stevens, was brutally attacked and murdered at the end of April, followed by another, who was the victim of an army-sponsored ambush in Bulawayo days later. When we heard the horrific account of how Martin Olds, a farmer and MDC supporter, suffered at the hands of 120 armed war veterans who had been bused to Bulwayo for the sole purpose of killing him, Dave made the decision to leave James and me with Mom while he returned to the farm. I was opposed to this idea, but at the same time, was also afraid to put James in any danger. Kimi's mother, Susie, wanted her home, understandably, so that she could have all her children together as she made her plans. The Parliamentary elections of June 2000 promised to be an intense time of aggression and violence, and Dave did not want us there. He and Kimi left at the beginning of May, and James and I remained in High Point.

While I was safe and secure in the United States, my heart was in Zimbabwe, fearful for my husband, my family, my friends and my staff, not knowing what was happening to all of them. I struggled to reconcile my guilt and shame at being safely removed from the tempestuous scene I had conjured in my mind, while my friends were left to cope with the massive task of ensuring a fair election process in the Tengwe district, not to mention keeping themselves and their families safe from danger. Dave arrived back on the farm to news of the third white farmer's death. Tengwe had organized Reaction Units that responded to radio calls from neighbors and friends when squatter situations would get out of hand. A roster was created, dividing the district into wards, each group with a leader, much like their military days. During "call-outs," there could be up to thirty or forty farmers trying to negotiate with a mob of unreasonable war vets. "We want your farm," "You must leave your farm," and "This is my house" were the least threatening arguments from them. "We are going to cut your throat tonight," or "We are going to kill you and your family" were the more common threats.

As the election drew near, I felt more and more isolated from Tengwe, and hated being so far away. The media are never accurate as they report only the terribly frightful news, and of course that was all I could find. Dave was difficult to reach as the phones were off and on, as normal, until finally he called one day to say that he was in Harare and had booked a ticket to return to the U.S. for the election period and would bring James and me home afterwards. I was so excited and relieved at this news and even more so when he landed safely in North Carolina. He reported that MDC was confident about the election, and the support was strong and defiant, despite the political intimidation that persisted. He had held meetings with our employees to educate them on the issues at stake, the voting procedure and their rights. The most difficult thing was to convince them that their vote was private, as they had been told by ZANU-PF that the government could find out how individuals voted.

In the end, Mugabe made sure of his party's victory through a campaign based on terror and torture and by traditional election-rigging methods. Throughout the campaign, Mugabe promised the world to his supporters (free land, free houses, etc.) but was worried enough by the strong support MDC enjoyed, to go the extra mile and dispatched as many combatants as he could to ensure victory during the election. Road blocks were erected all over the countryside, where busloads of people could be searched, and if unable to produce a ZANU-PF membership card, they were beaten, tortured or raped. The list of registered voters contained thousands of dead people (who voted for ZANU-PF, of course) and pre-stuffed ballot boxes were other methods Mugabe used to make certain the outcome.

Tengwe, as a community, had worked together to bring about a fair election within the district, as did most farming communities around the country. As our friends later related stories from the voting days, it became apparent how such a critical election was "lost." Using a single homestead as a base, the farmers split up and tried to transport MDC polling agents to man each of the voting stations around the district. Over the two day voting period, voters experienced massive beatings, intimidation and abuse at the hands of ZANU-PF thugs sent out to the rural areas for that purpose. The polling agents were so outnumbered that their presence was insignificant. They were not allowed to go anywhere near the ballot boxes and were not allowed to participate in the counting process. When the results were announced, MDC was given fifty-seven seats in parliament, to ZANUs sixty-two. By law, Mugabe is allowed to appoint thirty seats himself, and the result gave ZANU-PF a comfortable majority.

There was no doubt that MDC swept the election, but it did not matter. What did matter, though, was the crushing disappointment and ensuing despondency that overcame the country as a whole. It was visible in the faces of the farm workers, the farmers, even the children. For the first time, these people had found the courage to stand up for themselves, suffered and sacrificed so much in doing so, only to fail in their crusade at the hands of oppression and tyranny. The farm workers were incredibly vulnerable at that time, as their jobs, homes and lives were at stake, and the mood shifted to a defeatist one. The writing was on the wall. Mugabe was prepared to go to any lengths to stay in power, and there was no reason to believe the presidential election in 2002 would be any different.

Dave and I returned after the election to this somber mood, and I found it extremely difficult to re-integrate into the community having been gone during such a pivotal time. I felt distanced from my friends, but Gill assured me that everyone was just very down and depressed. Mandy insisted I get involved again, and I helped cater a "Medieval Nights" party at the club, as the committee had decided Tengwe was in desperate need of a morale booster. It didn't really work, as we were all still overcast by the discouraging loss and the uncertainty of the road ahead.

The violence did not ebb, as there was much retribution directed at the MDC officials and campaigners, many of whom retreated to safe-houses in fear for their lives. The war veterans still terrorized the farm workers on the farms that had been invaded, and hassled the farmers with endless work stoppages and equipment tampering. Planting season rolled around, mercifully slowing down the number of conflicts as the crops were being put in the ground.

During the last half of 2000, the political scene was relatively quiet, and even though many farms had been designated with a Section 5 by this time, no one was really sure what it meant. Dendera and Katengwe farms had still not been listed, but that fact alone did not offer much solace as we suspected that it was just a matter of time. Every farmer filed the appropriate papers to contest the act legally, and no real time frame was given for what may or may not happen. So, as farmers do, we planted our crops and waited for the rains to begin.

Chapter 3

Despite the limbo mode our lives took on, we carried on, grasping to daily routine for comfort. James was two and a half years old and growing up to be a real barefooted farm boy. He had a Zimbabwean accent, spoke as much Shona as he did English, and ruled the house all on his own. My staff delighted in teaching James Shona words and sayings they knew I did not know, and would send him in to tell me something I could not understand, and giggled endlessly when I had to ask them to translate. Kimi was ten years old at this stage and growing into a gorgeous girl. She and James had a strong bond, and he idolized his big sister. Her weekends home with us were special times for all of us.

Serena and I carried on with Garden Club meetings, taking on another year's responsibility, and Mandy roped me in for another big catering job as it was the year-end club meeting and dinner. We finally decided to chair the Entertainment Committee together for that upcoming year at the club. I had found that catering was something I thoroughly enjoyed, and something I did fairly well. James was old enough to give me a little more free time, and I was in need of a distraction. The methodical planning and preparation was right up my alley. Mandy and I attacked the Entertainment Committee job with gusto. We planned theme parties every few months and put weeks of preparation into each one. With her artistic talent and several rolls of tobacco bale paper from Jamie, we were able to transform the club into different worlds. I challenged myself to cook foods relevant to each theme and to serve dishes out of the ordinary. (To be honest, this wasn't that hard to do as the diet in Zimbabwe is quite a plain, meat and potato regimen.) We organized live music as often as we could. Tengwe was fortunate that one of our community members, Stuart Walker, was also a fantastic musician who enjoyed playing for these club functions as much as we enjoyed dancing all night to his music.

Our first New Year's party in 2000 was a huge gamble, as it was the middle of the rainy season, and we decided to have an outdoor beach party. Dave helped out with truckloads of river sand from the farm that we dumped onto the lawn off the club veranda for a beach. Serena, who was in charge of the club gardens, was horrified at this as she was sure it would kill the grass. We promised we would remove the sand the day after the party and all would be fine! We built a grass hut for an outdoor bar, painted hundreds of fish and a huge underwater scene in the main hall, served a Caribbean meal of Jerk Chicken with Mango Salsa as the main dish, and everyone dressed in bathing suits and sarongs. I had spent hours making homemade "chipwiches" which we served right off an ice-cream trolley as the vendors do on the South African beaches. The weather held for us and the entire community danced under the stars on the beach that night until sunrise and then, of course, participated in the time-honored tradition of cricket – this time in our cossies!

That Christmas, Dave took me out to shoot my first kudu, a magnificent antelope with large, curled horns. A group was living on the farm, and while we enjoyed their beauty, we found that they had become hopelessly addicted to our tobacco crop. I was very excited to bag a kudu, but even more excited to phone Aubrey to tell him that mine was much bigger than the one he had shot on his last trip out. Because a kudu weighs eight hundred pounds, Dave was able to provide every family on the farm with meat, as we did every Christmas. We saved the filet for ourselves and took great pleasure in cooking that particular piece of venison. I had learned that game had to be properly hung in the cold room for at least ten days and then marinated for about two days. It was an absolute delicacy when prepared correctly. I experimented with all kinds of game. Warthog (a sweet pork), impala (a more tender, flavorful venison), kudu, francolin, and dove all found their way to our dining table on a regular basis.

I taught Louie many new recipes, but the ones he had of his own were some of the best foods I have ever had. He could make an oxtail stew we ate over sadza (corn meal - the staple diet of the Africans) that was so delicious he became famous in Tengwe for it. He made peri-peri dove breasts that melted in your mouth. (Peri-peri is a Portuguese word for spicy and a common flavoring in Southern Africa) I still have yet to roast potatoes with an outer crust like he could. I was able to show him how to make a good spaghetti, homemade bread, salads and salad dressings. He could not read or write, so everything had to be done from memory. As with most cooks in Zimbabwe, his repertoire was fairly basic, but he did improve drastically during our time together. Because I enjoy the kitchen, we often shared the cooking duties, unlike many women who preferred their cooks do it all. I must admit I became very spoiled by never having to clean and prep vegetables, or wash dishes.

Chapter 4

As we put the year 2000 to bed, we all had to believe better days were ahead, but it was not to be. James turned three right around the time our great friend Meyer was diagnosed with pancreatic cancer. He had been increasingly sick for some time, but the doctors in Harare were unable to determine the cause, and by the time the cancer was found, the tumor was massive. A trip to doctors in Johannesburg confirmed Gill and Meyer's worst fears. He was untreatable. The community took this news very badly. In addition to the crushing news, they faced an incredible mountain of medical expenses. Their closest friends held a meeting to organize donations from many in the community, which helped alleviate a lot of their stress. This was the common reaction when friends were in trouble. In the early years of the community, the Tengwe Cactus Fund was established as a growing fund to be used in emergency cases around the community. Sharon Kockott took this kind-hearted fundraising to a new level as she organized a black-tie affair every two years dedicated solely to benefit three or four recipients. Again, it was a team effort that required help from everyone to pull off this elegant affair, and the Cactus Fund benefit became one of our most anticipated events.

A bizarre series of events then unfolded. The Moolmans heard about an alternative medicine guru in Guatemala and made a desperate decision to seek his help. The ironic thing was that Aubrey had proposed to his girlfriend, Saskia, just before Christmas. Her family is from Guatemala, and the wedding was scheduled for May, 2001, in Guatemala. Until Aubrey announced his plans, I don't think anyone in Tengwe had any idea where Guatemala was. Then, all of a sudden, Gill and Meyer were on their way there hoping for miracles, and Dave and I were on our way there for my brother's wedding. Sadly, in the end, they did not get the miracle they needed, and Meyer died the night of Aubrey's rehearsal dinner. Dave and I were so fortunate to have seen our dear friend the days before he died, as they had been away from Tengwe for three months by the time we arrived for the wedding. Our hearts were heavy for our friends, but we celebrated Aubrey and Saskia's marriage at a stunning setting in Antigua, Guatemala.

We had a very good crop and good rains that season, but the farm invasions were on the rise again. It seemed that the war veterans were more determined than ever to see Mugabe's plan through. This increased wave of activity brought with it a renewed feeling of hopelessness and skepticism regarding the future, culminating with another one thousand farms that were listed that June, 2001. We did not escape this sweep of designations and saw Dendera and Katengwe join the ranks of listed farms. By this time, it was not as traumatic and shocking to be listed, because almost the whole of the country was now on the list. All the same, I got a terrible pit in my stomach when I saw our farms in black and white in Mugabe's paper. I couldn't help thinking "What have we done to deserve this?"

My anger and outrage at the injustice of it all was matched only by my frustration at how utterly helpless we were. I began putting off projects around the house. A stack of pictures intended to be framed accumulated in my office. I could not get motivated to put new plants in the garden, thinking I would not see them grow. The new rose bed I had intended to develop was filled with old wildflower seeds instead. I had about fifty rose bushes at that time and still found much fulfillment in them, but I couldn't justify the expense of the new bushes. More than that, I could not bear the thought of having to abandon my beauties. The question mark that clouded our future forced us to consider our alternatives, something that at that time seemed next to impossible. I could not envision another life for us. Where would we go and what would we do? These were the questions that usually stumped us, and most times the discussion would end with, "Let's wait and see."

I also could not bear the thought of taking James away from his home. Dave had arranged for a little boy named Shamisu, (a son of Shirley's cook) who was about ten, to be James' official playmate every day. James and Shamisu ran around the yard all day long, the best of friends despite the age gap. His favorite game at this stage was reversing toy cars, trailers and boats into a man-made dam in the driveway. Never or Shamisu would dig a hole in the dirt about five feet in diameter and about one foot deep, fill it with water, and James would play there all day, launching boats and reversing trailers in and out of the water. Another activity James and Shamisu did was to "go hunting." I would pack a cooler with cokes and snacks, and they would take toy guns and trek all around the yard and the barns next to the house, "shooting" birds. Shamisu came to be part of the family. We took him to Kariba, I took him to the club to look after James, we fed him and I slipped him money every now and then. Shamisu was the only reason James began riding a two-wheeler bike at age three. One day, I had Never clean out a storage shed in the yard, and we came across Kimi's old pink two-wheeler. James saw that this was bigger and more exciting than his smaller and shorter bike which was burdened with training wheels. He insisted Shamisu hold the back of the seat steady, while James pedaled all over the yard with Shamisu running behind, keeping him balanced. Irene came to me a few hours later to say, "Madam, come and see James. He rides the bike alone!"

Sure enough, from that day, we discarded all training wheels. I certainly would not have had the patience and stamina to do what Shamisu did. James was quite bossy with him at times, but I suppose he picked up on the pecking order around the house enough to think that Shamisu worked for him. Shamisu, at that time, was not in school because his parents could not afford it, and when Shirley heard this, she paid for his schooling. James then had to settle for his playmate on the weekends and during the holidays, which he was not at all happy about.

One day, all the dogs were barking wildly, alerting me that a strange car had arrived in my driveway. I walked outside to see three people, two men and a woman, walking towards the house. "We have come to evaluate your house for the government," was their greeting. We had heard that this was going on around the area, and Dave had told me if they did come, to just let them do their job. So I did, but watched with amusement as they tried to measure the length of the house with an old cloth measuring tape. They drew an elementary diagram of the house in pencil on a yellow legal pad, made an incomplete list of the number of doors, windows and light fittings in the house, and then attempted to measure the fencing around the entire garden. Having no proper tool to do this, they asked me how many meters I thought it was. Of course I said I had no idea. They spent the entire day on our farm, doing the same sort of calculations at the barns, the workshops, Shirley and Andy's house, Timot's house, and the sheds. There were rumors that the government would pay farmers for the improvements to the land, if not for the land itself. These teams of surveyors were sent to evaluate the farms. I can see now that the government never had any intention of paying us at all, and those estimations were such a joke anyway that none of them could have come close to being accurate. In real market terms before all the land invasions, the farm had been evaluated in 1998 at about $500,000 U.S. dollars.

Zimbabwe is an incredible breeding ground for rumors, and certainly at that time, there were so many rumors floating around that no one knew what to believe. Our moods shifted up and down with all the news, and we rode an emotional roller coaster unlike any I have known. Any little piece of good news could brighten a day, and the bad news sent us all scrambling to the club for a meeting and drinks to drown our sorrows.

Dave put seed beds in that July, but was not sure he would actually plant a crop that season. In light of all the Section 5 notices, banks had become very hesitant to finance the large sums of money necessary for a tobacco crop. If the government was going to acquire the farms, what could the banks hold as collateral? Many farmers, especially those with active war vets on the property, were unable to secure loans for the upcoming season. Inflation had escalated at such a rate that the cost of a crop was prohibitive, to say the least. With a crippled currency, a farm we weren't sure we owned and a presidential election around the corner, we could not be assured that we would even be able to sell our crop. Once again, we said we would "wait and see." We could always sell our seedlings.

Chapter 5

I busied myself with preparations for my family's visit in August.
Mom, eager to see her grandson, arrived in July, and Aubrey and his new
wife, Saskia, arrived a few weeks later in August. Dave had gone to Harare
to meet their plane and called to say he was on his way home, when an "All
Call" announcement came over my radio to inform us that massive rioting
and looting had broken out in Chinhoyi and that the town was shut down.
Many cars driving through had been stoned by a mob of about one hundred,
and twelve farmers had been illegally arrested for attacking the war veterans,
when really they were trying to protect their friends from the mob.
Fortunately, Dave had not gotten too far out of Harare where his cell phone
would have lost signal, and I was able to stop him. They ended up having to
stay the night in Harare before driving to the farm the next day.

Even though tensions were high at the time, we managed to entertain
my family and give them the unique African experience, maybe even a little
more than they bargained for. During supper one night, the radio rang and
Dave had to leave for a call-out. The war veterans had gotten out of hand at
our friend Leon's farm, and he needed back-up. Despite Aubrey's curiosity,
Dave would not let him tag along. I was not too concerned as this was a
fairly regular occurrence those days, but still waited anxiously for his call to
say all was well and he would be home soon. It took several hours, but the

radio finally rang at about ten o'clock and Dave was on his way. At ten-thirty, there was still no sign of Dave. I radioed him again and again but could not get an answer. By midnight I was frantic, when finally he called again to say he was almost home. Of course, my imagination had played out a million horrible scenes in my head, and when Dave related what had gone on at Leon's, I realized that I was not far off.

Dave and two other farmers found themselves confronted with a war veteran leader and about thirty of his men, drunk and wielding poles and axes. They were on a real power trip, and wanted to show the workers on that farm that they were in charge, not the farmer. They said to Dave, "Three white men are going to die tonight." It was a sticky situation and Dave later told me that he had never felt so threatened, and at one point really did believe that he might, in fact, be killed. The head war veteran, named Tim Sicha, was notorious in the area for his violent tendencies. It took hours of negotiating to diffuse the situation, but they did and were about to leave when another group arrived out of the bushes, and the whole thing started over. He had already called me and put the radio away when the second group arrived. Fortunately, Dave has such a strong command of the Shona language and culture and can speak to them as an equal that they were able to get out of that situation unharmed.

Shortly after that, I was the only customer at the butchery one afternoon and felt two men glaring at me as I bought some drinks. As I walked to my car, they came on either side of me, threatening to "take me," "take my husband's farm" and that "things were going to change." I was suddenly frightened, even though it was the middle of the day in the open and hurried to get in my car. They let me be, laughing at my obvious fear, but I was quite shaken.

Enough incidents like these and horrific stories of violence from all farming districts caused us to seriously look at our lives and question what we were doing there. I was no longer able to walk the farm with the dogs on my own anymore, for fear of who I could meet on the road. Many of the employees had gone over to ZANU-PF in order to save their lives, and some even with hopes of maybe getting a farm for themselves. We couldn't really blame them, but we couldn't really know who we could trust anymore either. We began speaking in hushed tones around the house regarding our plans, what was discussed at Farmer's Association meetings or politics in general. I hated the rift Mugabe had created between the races. The suspicion and mistrust that had been instilled in some of the farm employees was certainly not there when I arrived in Zimbabwe, but over time, Mugabe had hammered his message of hatred home so many times that many began to believe him. After the long and tortuous campaign, many simply gave up the fight and gave in to ZANU pressures. I naively assumed my staff would be loyal, and was shocked to learn that Louie had pegged a plot with the war veterans on our neighbor's farm. After thinking about it for a while, I realized that he, too, had to look out for his family's best interests for the future as well. The mental toll the situation took on us all was too much to bear at times.

The economic decline throughout the country affected our lives in every way on a day to day basis. Fuel shortages were rampant, and farming communities were forced to order fuel in bulk, and then distribute it among the farmers when it was their turn. As a result, fuel conservation meant fewer trips to Harare, the kids came home less on weekends, and fishing trips were cut in half. We had to plan ahead for a weekend trip to Kariba, so that we had enough diesel to get us there and back and enough petrol for the boat. It became the norm to travel with huge containers, or "chigubus," of fuel wherever we went. Inflation was escalating at such a rate that a $500 note was introduced, although by the time it entered circulation, we needed a $1000 note, or higher. Lack of foreign exchange made imported specialty items scarce and expensive. I still insisted on buying things like Kellogg cereals, Nescafe coffee and South African wines whenever I could find them. The local goods were OK in a pinch, but I was accustomed to the imported flavors. The grocery stores, in order to hide the fact that so many items were unavailable, began filling the empty shelves with cheap, one-ply loo roll. It was not uncommon to find two or three aisles of just toilet paper on some days!

I had arranged a surprise for Dave's birthday that August. Sharon and Andy had a magnificent hunting camp on the Zambezi River in Chirundu, the border town between Zambia and Zimbabwe. Situated right on the tall banks of the river in amongst the thorn trees, it was a unique spot that offered fantastic fishing and game viewing. They were kind enough to let us use the camp, and I invited all our friends to celebrate Dave's birthday with my family on the river. Our group totaled about thirty, including kids. Those who didn't fit in the five permanent lodges brought tents that housed the rest of the group, dubbed "Tent City." We spent the first day parked on the sandbank in the middle of the river, swimming, fishing, and horsing around, watching the elephant, hippo and crocodiles all around us. This was just one of many occasions that highlighted all the great aspects of our life. A day spent with best friends in a magical setting like the Zambezi River could easily wash away all our thoughts of ever leaving home and make us forget all the hassles that existed in our lives. On these days, Dave and I would look at each other, shake our heads and say, "How can we even *think* about leaving this place?" We knew that we would never find a life like that anywhere else in the world and doubted that even a suitable replacement existed.

We did have a strong dose of reality to remind us where we were, for the next morning I detected stress in camp when I heard Andy yelling for Usef, the camp cook. Dave went to see what had happened, and it turned out the camp had been robbed that night while we slept hard after a long night of partying. Mom lost everything, and the folks in "Tent City" were also victims of the looting. It certainly put a damper on our weekend, but we all knew that common robbery is an inherent part of life in Africa that just had to be dealt with.

After my family left, Dave and I knew we had to sit down and make some decisions. I was so torn inside about what I wanted for us, and I know he was as well. We were trying to take into consideration our responsibilities as parents, as employers and as children. What about Kimi? What about Shirley and Andy? What about our employees? And then of course, the most confusing question - what about us? What would we do for a living? What about immigration? Could we be happy without our friends?

Around this time, the Commonwealth conference was held in Nigeria, where leaders from Britain, Canada, Nigeria, South Africa, Australia and Kenya held a summit meeting to discuss the situation in Zimbabwe. The news that elated us was that Mugabe had agreed to call off all land invasions, remove the war veterans from the farms and de-list a majority of the designated farms. We grasped to this news like a life preserver, in hopes that everything could go back to normal. Once again, we climbed on our emotional roller coaster as the war veterans refused to accept the Abuja Agreement, and Mugabe set in place the new "Fast Track" land scheme, to hurry the process of acquiring our farms. This was not the first time Mugabe had deliberately snubbed and defied international pressure and would certainly not be the last.

In light of all this, Dave and I made a decision not to grow a crop that year. We chose to travel around South Africa and America, and just see what it might be like to live somewhere else. Deep down, we hoped that maybe something might change for the better in our absence, and we could resume our lives. In reality, we were just putting our lives on hold for a year, prolonging our state of limbo. Andy had decided to grow a small crop in a desperate attempt to boost their savings, as their substantial retirement fund had more than halved in value because of the hyperinflation and decline of the Zimbabwe dollar. Many of the older generation suffered this circumstance and were as bewildered as any about what the future held. Looking back now, I can see we were all sort of operating as though in a daze, repeating the chant of the times, "Hopefully things will come right," and desperately clinging to the dying dream that somehow we would be left alone to continue with our lives.

Dave and I were fortunate that we could embark on our ventures. James was almost four, not in school yet, and a good age to travel. We left the farm the first of November for the first of many long drives on what was to be an incredible journey through South Africa.

Chapter 6

We had been to Ballito, a resort town on the east coast near Durban, the prior year, but South Africa has so much to offer and is so vast, that I was extremely eager to see as much as we could. Having spent so much time as a young man hunting and guiding in parts of South Africa, Dave was happy to be able to share that part of his life with us. We did not have any set timetables, except that I had rented a flat in Cape Town for the last week of November. We needed to make our way there by that time, but otherwise we were open to what we wanted to do. It is a wonderful way to travel, especially with a child.

As soon as we crossed the border at Beitbridge, the stress faded away and we all began to relax. We were successful in exiting the country with a large amount of foreign exchange, a risk we were always willing to take in order to beef up our savings account in South Africa. We found clever and ingenious ways to hide cash throughout the car and luggage in case of a search. Our first stops included Kruger National Park and the wildlife areas surrounding it. South Africa is famous for its Bed and Breakfast spots, as these are far more common than hotels. Our travel book listed all of them, and we hopped from one lovely setting to the next, meeting a variety of interesting people along the way. We spent a few days in Durban with Cheryl and Dean Barnes. We relished the chance to relax and forget our troubles for a time at the beaches of Umshlonga Rocks on the east coast. The Garden Route of South Africa was our next adventure, and we began in East London and stopped along the way in charming coastal towns of St. Francis Bay, Knysna, Wilderness and Hermanus. It was in Knysna where Dave and I wanted to stop and set up house. We fell in love with this unique place for its beauty and diversity. The B&B we chose overlooked Kynsa from a steep hill over the water, and was actually for sale, though way out of our range. The possibility of running a place like that was something we entertained for many months. With Dave's guiding abilities and my catering skills, we thought it was something that we could manage as a profession if we were going to have to leave the farm.

We enjoyed fantastic whale watching in Hermanus before landing in Camps Bay in Cape Town. I had not seen water that blue and inviting since Mozambique and was instantly intrigued by the vibrancy and energy of Cape Town. We extended our stay for as many days as we could afford.

Before heading back towards Zimbabwe, we stopped for a few days in the wine country and again decided that this was a place where we would like to run a B&B. Franschoek stole our hearts, but we enjoyed drinking wine all over Stellenbosch and Paarl. Gill's daughter, Nita, who was at the University of Stellenbosch, a gorgeous and immaculate campus, led us to some of the college students' haunts. These mainly consisted of the vineyards that allowed the most glasses of wine for the least amount of money.

The drive from Cape Town to Johannesburg took two days through the Karoo, a desolate place. We spent the night just before the border in Peitersberg at a popular stopover place for traveling Zimbabweans called the Ranch Motel, where we happened to bump into some families from Tengwe on their way down for a holiday. We had been gone for almost six weeks, and they remarked on how relaxed and stress-free we looked to them. In contrast, I could see the marks and wear of strife on their faces. They did not have much good news to share, for things had not improved at all since our departure. This did not come as a surprise to us, as the South African papers were full of the news of Zimbabwe. The unstable politics affected the entire region. While Thabo Mbeki, the president of South Africa, would not publicly condemn Mugabe's tactics, he was under much pressure to try to mitigate the effects of all the bad press.

Re-entry at the Zimbabwean border brought back all the old concerns and worries we had so eagerly left behind. Our time away allowed us to contemplate our future, but as our backs were not entirely against the wall yet, no absolute decisions had to be made. We were prepared to enjoy the Christmas and New Years' season with our friends and family and looked forward to our lengthy stay in the States to begin in January 2002.

The first social event upon our return from South Africa was the aforementioned Garden Club AGM. As I described, it was one for the books. Mandy and I decided the New Years' Eve theme would celebrate our beloved country and chose a true African theme. She outdid herself with stunning murals of sunsets and wildlife scenes. We brought in my kudu and duiker horns to adorn the bar, flame lilies and proteas for the tables, and served a meal of traditional fare. It was a fairly festive time, but a heavy sadness was in the air that New Year's Eve as we missed our friend Meyer, and so much tension and anxiety lay directly beneath the surface of our lives.

Dave, James and I left the farm mid-January after Kimi had gone back to school, and arrived in North Carolina. We celebrated James' 4th birthday in High Point with Mom before we took off for Florida, where we spent the month of February. We had often entertained thoughts of Dave becoming a fishing guide somehow, somewhere, and wanted to check out the scene in Florida and the Keys. Friends had arranged a few fishing trips for Dave while we were there, and we quickly realized that it is quite a difficult profession to break into. We had a super holiday in the sun and on the beach with James, but were ready to stop traveling for a while.

Upon returning to High Point, the news from Zimbabwe was not at all encouraging. Lead-up to the presidential election to take place at the end of March was as violent as ever. Mugabe was once again setting his agenda to steal another election at any cost, farm invasions were on the rise and MDC followers continued to fear for their lives. Not surprisingly, Mugabe won the election he rigged.

In our original travel plan, Jamie and Mandy were to join us in April, and we were going to Disney with all the kids. After the disappointment of the election and the increasing ambivalence that controlled our lives, all plans were cancelled. Dave and I decided to save our money and stay put in North Carolina for the rest of our time. Once again, we had nothing but time to consider our future, and once again, we could not bring ourselves to come to any solid conclusions.

We returned to Zimbabwe the first week of May, only to be dealt a staggering blow. On May 10, 2002, Mugabe issued mass Section 8 notices, by way of the *Daily Herald*, which would force all but a handful of white farmers off their farms. The Section 5 notices had lost their grandeur and had been usurped by the dreaded Section 8 notice, the one that *really* meant your farm was gone. According to this new law, we had ninety days – August 8, 2002 being the deadline – to vacate our farms and homes or we would be arrested for trespassing. I wept at this news. I surprised myself by this reaction, for we knew it was surely inevitable that we would make this next list, but for me, that last sliver of hope had truly been destroyed.

Not everyone agreed as to what would actually happen. Some chose to ignore the notice, daring and defying the government to take their land. Dave was convinced they were for real, and we finally made the agonizing decision to leave Zimbabwe. We concluded that South Africa would not be a good decision, as it was also susceptible to political and economic instability, and we were quite wary of African politics by that time. The United States would be our new home.

Chapter 7

That decision brought an onslaught of more difficult decisions. What about Kimi? What about our workers and their families? What about the dogs? Where do we go first? What will we do? What about immigration? What about our stuff?

The next three months were devoted to selling all that we could – cars, boats, motorbikes, etc. Once again my steadfast friends came to my rescue and helped me organize a house sale. We had discovered that we could only ship a one cubic meter crate out of the country without income tax clearance, a huge expense and something we flatly refused to pay to the very government that had stolen our lives. I was then faced with condensing my house down to one cubic meter! Where would you start? China, silver, photos, sentimental items, some of my nicer linen, CDs, artwork, a favorite table and a rug quickly filled my limited space and was shipped to the U.S. The rest of our household and personal belongings were sold at the house sale or given away. I tried to give each of my good friends something special that would remind them of us. I gave Debbie all my beautiful white serving platters she always admired and the champagne glasses we had toasted with at our wedding. I gave Mandy and Jamie my stereo to remember all the dancing and good times we had shared. I insisted that Sue and Serena come dig up my most prosperous rose bushes. Serena had taught me a saying that "If you don't give your garden away, it will die." So many times I would get a clipping from someone for my garden, only to have them come to me the following season needing some back as their specimen had a problem. How could I now not give back what she had given me so generously years earlier? I bequeathed my wedding hat to Gill's daughter Nita, and encouraged all the Tengwe girls to wear it in their weddings.

The day of my house sale was one of the most emotionally exhausting days I have ever had. All of my beautiful furniture that we had collected over the years, electrical appliances and personal items right down to shoes and spoons were sold. I watched as my friends bought items, excited about how they would use them or where they would put them. All the while my mind was filled with regret and insecurity – "Have I done the right thing? What if they **don't** take the farms after all?" I fought jealous tinges while my friends packed my things in their cars.

All the while we were taking our time packing and sorting out our things, we knew we were actually fortunate to have that luxury. Every day we heard stories of families in other districts not too far from us who had been given two hours to clear out of their homes. Thugs arrived in large groups, armed and ready to fight, claiming ownership of farms and homes. Most of these people were lucky to escape with their children and pets, not to mention their lives.

Chapter 8

Kimi, age twelve, was another concern we faced. After much
discussion, Dave and Susie decided that she would move to the U.S. with us.
With the perfect vision of hindsight, I can now say that we all should have
known that this was a disastrous decision that never should have been made.
In our defense, as parents, we were simply trying to do what seemed best for
the future of our children during a tense time.

Our plane tickets were booked for mid-August. I was to take Kimi,
James and Ellie, and go to Mom's house first. The other dogs had all been
adopted by various friends, except for Sam who was too old and deaf, and
had to be put down. We had chosen Wilmington, NC, for our home, as we
had some friends and contacts there, and the coastal location appealed to us.
Dave would fly a month later, as Andy needed help wrapping up business on
the farm. There was so much to take care of, it was overwhelming. June and
July were hectic, uncertain months for us all. We spent a family vacation at
Kariba, not knowing when we would ever do that again. We attended a
series of farewell dinner parties, and received special gifts from our friends.
By the time our final party came at the club, I was an emotional wreck.
When we walked into the bar and saw how it had been decorated with red,
white and blue ribbons and U.S. flags, I burst into tears. I gave a speech, but

could barely talk for the tears, and then listened to Dave speak. I realized then for the first time how apprehensive he was about our move. I listened as he spoke of how he regretted that James would not have the wonderful childhood he did and that he would not know his family's farm. I left that party and those friends knowing I was leaving behind a vital part of myself, and it was excruciating and terrifying. We did not, and could not, know the strife that was ahead of us, but we were going to have to face it without the sturdy pillars of support we had depended on for so long.

Chapter 9

We arrived at Mom's exhausted and fearful. I think of all of us, Ellie was as bewildered as any. The new smells and surroundings had her totally confused, and she looked at me in horror when I put a leash around her neck for the first time! I was able to buy a car, rent a house in Wilmington, and enroll the children into schools in the month before Dave arrived. In those first few weeks in the States, I anxiously discerned that life was going to be vastly more expensive than I had originally thought. By the time we were lined up with medical insurance, schooling, rent and all the other essentials, I was horrified to see what our monthly costs would be. By comparison, our financial position would be far more modest than we had experienced on the farm. In Zimbabwe, we were able to own two Toyota Landcruisers, and here we could not afford one. The yearly trips overseas and frequent local holidays that had been in our grasp were now beyond reach. As we had been forced to abandon our household goods and furniture, we needed to furnish a house. I will be forever grateful to Mom and our great friends in High Point, who organized almost an entire house of second-hand furniture for us.

Communication with Dave was difficult during that time as he and Andy had cleared off the farm over the weekend of the evacuation date. Many farmers experienced horrific and violent scenes during those next weeks. It turned out that the government was, in fact, serious about taking the farms. Over the course of the next year, hundreds of farmers relocated. Harare was full to the brim with farmers living in town flats, waiting to see of they could go home again. Many families took the same course we did, and while many are still in Zimbabwe, our friends stretch from Australia, New Zealand, England, to the United States and South Africa.

Andy and Shirley were to retreat to Cheryl's house in Durban, planning to stay there indefinitely until some other arrangements could be made. By the time Andy and Dave had actually vacated the farm, they had been threatened with arrest several times. On hearing that the police were coming to find them, the two men stealthily snuck off to the Zambezi River for a last bit of father-son fishing in their homeland. There is no place like the African bush to hide if you really need to! By the time Dave left the farm for good, he said our house was a mere shell and his parents house had been given over to nine "A2 settlers," meaning the first line of war vets who stood to gain from these invasions. Goats and pigs grazed in the garden and ruined Shirley's magnificent oasis. Eventually we heard that our house had also been given over to the same number of people. I tormented myself with images of those men in my house. The fittings, fixtures and all things of value would have been stripped first, and the doors would have been used for firewood. What could have gone through their minds as they destroyed the very door where I marked my son's growth?

Dave arrived the third week of September, and I was so relieved to have him safely with us. Kimi was already missing her mother, brother and sister terribly, but Dave's presence calmed her a bit. She had entered the seventh grade, and I realize now that being a twelve-year-old girl is tough and unfair, even during the very best of circumstances. We were all trying to find our feet in a new way of life and culture, and she struggled hopelessly to adapt without the support of her mom. James mourned his dam and his home, and tore at my heart when he asked everyday for months, "When are we going back to my farm?"

Leading up to our departure, we tried to turn everything we could into US dollars, but we arrived with less than we needed to survive for long without employment. I had started a small catering business that trickled along, and as we researched the expensive and slow-moving immigration routes we would have to follow, it became clear that Dave could not work for some months. By Thanksgiving of that year, we were all severely depressed. Of all the difficult times in my life, that is without a doubt the darkest year I have ever known. We physically ached for our old lives, and could not find a way to soothe the pain. I cried almost daily, as did Kimi. James had age on his side, as he was beginning to forget the past. At times, I wished I could forget just so that I wouldn't feel the loss so intensely. I watched Dave suffer silently and knew he was hurting even more than I was.

There were some good times as well – exciting new traditions like Halloween and Thanksgiving distracted the kids, and living at the beach was a novelty. Eventually we managed to have some social life, but nothing like we had enjoyed in the past. There truly is no substitute for your best friends. Even though I was "home," it sure didn't feel like it. I felt as much a stranger as Dave a lot of the time and once again had to overcome the insecurities of yet another different world. I reluctantly admitted that I was quite naïve in thinking we could easily transfer our family to the American way of life without casualties. I discovered huge disappointment in the fact that I could not truly relate to many of my old friends and came to realize that I had grown and matured in a different manner.

Kimi became more and more unhappy, and we began to dread the Sunday telephone calls to Susie, as that was usually what sent her into uncontrollable sobs. Dave was desperate over her situation, and after Christmas, we decided that she would return to Zimbabwe with her mother. It was undoubtedly the right decision, but possibly the most painful thing

Dave has ever endured. He put Kimi on the plane back to Africa the morning we celebrated James' fifth birthday.

Over the next few months, we realized that it would be very difficult for Dave to find work. It was extremely frustrating to know how talented and resourceful he is, but his qualities do not translate into this job market. Having just entered into the Iraq war, the American economy and job market were unsteady at best at that time. Spring passed with Dave obtaining odd jobs – mostly manual labor and tractor driving. I could not stand to see this capable, talented man reduced to doing the work of his former workers. Was this some sort of sick irony?

That summer, we visited a business broker and eventually found a small business that we could buy, with Mom's help, and run for ourselves. By the time all the negotiations had taken place, eighteen months had passed since we had arrived and our savings account had dwindled down to a frightening level. That situation alone scared me to death and kept me from sleep most nights, but at least we had something to sink our teeth into and could get down to work.

We ran a little transportation business that catered to the exclusive clientele of a resort island off the coast of North Carolina. It was seasonal and not a lot of money, but just enough for us to live on. With the purchase of that company, we began the long, uphill struggle of rebuilding our shattered lives.

Epilogue

As I write this epilogue, we are now at yet another crossroad in our lives. We ran that transportation company successfully for four years, and sold it six months ago for a small profit. With Aubrey's help, we were able to buy a moderate house several years ago. We are as settled as we can be, but far from fulfilled. Starting over has meant living a completely different kind of life, one that places us in a lower and more humble lifestyle than before. In Zimbabwe, that never mattered – not so in the first world. As we now search for a new direction, we are still hoping to find a way back to Africa in some capacity. Dave has recently confided in me that Africa, and not necessarily Zimbabwe, is the only place he can truly survive.

We were able to go back to Zimbabwe in December 2006 for a month for Christmas. It was my first trip back, Dave's second. I was so emotionally torn that I had to shelve the writing of this book for one year. It truly was an amazing trip. Most importantly, it was a chance for us to show James the life, land and people he had heard us talk about for so long, as well as a chance to reunite with family and friends. He did not remember anything from his early days but had the time of his life during that vacation. We divided our time between Kariba and Harare. He reconnected with his sister, and re-made the friends from his childhood, bridging the culture gap in the way only children can do. Despite the four years I had been away, I picked right up with my friends and wallowed gleefully in the ease and comfort of those relationships. I left Zimbabwe, once again in massive tears, feeling the same heart-wrenching feelings I had felt the first time I had to leave all that I loved behind.

Zimbabwe, the country, has suffered endlessly at the hands of Robert Mugabe and continues to spiral into pandemonium. Life has almost reverted to the dark ages – water, electricity and basic food items are rare commodities. Only a handful of white farmers are left, and they continue to be harassed. Inflation has reached 100,000%, or some off-the-wall figure like it, and continues to climb. The Zimbabwean dollar trades at eighteen million to one U.S. dollar on the black market and loses value daily. The thousands of once prosperous farms, millions of acres, now lie uncultivated and overgrown while the majority of the population starves. Robert Mugabe and his cronies bask in wealth, seemingly immune to the fact that they have destroyed what was once the "Bread Basket of Africa." Many of the ZANU-PF cabinet ministers who claimed the elite farms for themselves practically enslave their workers, paying and feeding them inconsistently at best. Not surprisingly, the war vets who live on the farms are the worst, many times telling the employees that in return for their work, they are actually allowed to live in their homes. Somehow, the brave and resourceful people of Zimbabwe continue to "make a plan" and carry on, forever indulging in their enduring optimism that things may change.

Kimi moved to Cape Town a couple of years ago and is very happy and settled as she prepares for her eighteenth birthday this year. We see her about once a year, either here or in Africa. Shirley and Andy, now in their late seventies, have recently relocated to England where they face the difficult challenges of a new society and way of life.

When I examine each of us individually to see how we have

weathered the storm, I see very different people from the ones I see in Chapter One. In his meticulous, patient and steadfast way, Dave has proven his worth in a world that he never believed he was suited for and has regained some of his confidence. He has earned the deserved respect of a diehard fishing community, for he can now out-fish most of the "good ole boys" here. Even though we saw the arduous process of obtaining citizenship through, and he has his American passport, he will never feel like an American and will never feel at home anywhere but in Africa. His determined effort to settle in the U.S. has been a valiant one, but this is not a world that harmonizes with his soul. He passionately longs for what he still calls home, and I do not fault him or blame him for it, for many days so do I.

James has flourished into a clever, well-behaved ten-year old boy. He is settled in his life and is one of the most popular boys at school. Ellie has never been so comfortable, as she now sleeps in our bed and will never consider sleeping outside again.

As for me, I am no longer a young girl, but a grown woman more prepared than ever to face whatever life throws my way. I have learned many things over the past five years, or at least things that apply to the way I view life. There is a saying in Zimbabwe, "Don't lose the plot," meaning don't lose sight of what is true and real. I have learned that what is true and real for us is our friends and our family, not a measure of success or wealth. We may struggle to make ends meet, but we feel far richer than the wealthiest in so many ways.

I know that Dave and I together can overcome obstacles, large or small. I know that we have a solid relationship that has withstood the toughest tests a marriage can endure. I also know that the years I spent in Zimbabwe were the best of my life. I used to grieve the fact that at age thirty-seven, my best years are now behind me. I do not grieve anymore for I have come to realize how incredibly fortunate I am to have known the special life and the community that I did, no matter how brief. I can now embrace those times and am able to carry that experience with me and draw strength from it in so many ways.

I know that I will need to draw on that strength once more, possibly sooner rather than later, in order to retrace our steps. The lure of Africa is much like a riptide, and we know that in order to save our lives, and our happiness, we must not fight it.

Breinigsville, PA USA
22 February 2010
232990BV00004B/20/P